Secrets o

Mentally Tough Athlete

First published in 2014 by

David James Publishing

www.davidjamespublishing.com

www.drmarkselliott.co.uk

ISBN: 978-0-9575610-9-0

Secrets of the Mentally Tough Athlete

60 World-class strategies to transform your sports performance from the inside out

Dr. Mark S. Elliott

Foreword by **MICHAEL HOEY,** Multiple European Tour Winner

Dedication

This book is dedicated to my two sons, James and Matthew. I love you both very much - the best sons a man could ever wish for. Dream big, work hard, live, and love!

To my beautiful wife, Alison - the surprised woman behind her man's success - thank you so much for your unstinting support during the writing of the book... and for everything.

This book is also for the athletes of the world who struggle to silence the white noise of an untrained mind. Take heart, you are just a few pages away from discovering how to do it!

About the Author

Dr. Mark Elliott is a highly respected sport psychologist, author and speaker. His ground-breaking 'Mental Monster Model' has helped transform ordinary performers into extraordinary ones and world-beaters. His approach to developing mental toughness has enabled many well-known professional and elite amateur athletes and teams achieve huge goals and sporting success. Clients include European Tour golfers, British & Irish Lions' rugby players; Olympic and Paralympic athletes; professional football and ice hockey teams; senior county teams and individual performers in Gaelic sports; and, tennis players, swimmers and boxers.

Mark is a BPS Chartered and HCPC-registered Sport and Exercise Psychologist, and an Associate Fellow of the British Psychological Society. He is a regular contributor to the print and broadcast media and authored the bestselling sport psychology book *Facing Frankenstein - Defeat Your True Opponent in Sport*.

Heavily in demand, Mark divides his professional work between consultancy, writing and speaking. He lives in Dromore, County Down, with his wife Alison and sons, James and Matthew.

drmarkselliott.co.uk

Acknowledgements

I would like to offer my sincere thanks to David Stokes, Jim Montgomery and the many people behind the scenes at David James Publishing for their unwavering support and input throughout the writing, editing and publication of this book.

Special thanks to Michael Hoey for writing the Foreword to the book and for contributing to several of its Secrets. The golfing world can be yours Mike; that's how talented you are!

I will be forever grateful to all of the athletes referred to in this book, and to the hundreds upon hundreds of sports performers I've had the pleasure to work with and help over the past two decades. Thank you so much. The learning was mutual, believe me!

A heartfelt thanks to the wonderful illustrator and artist, Adrian Lutton, for his graphic design work on the book.

I simply cannot complete the Acknowledgements without saying a posthumous "thank you" to Mary Shelley, who, through her Gothic novel *Frankenstein; or, The Modern Prometheus*, gave the world a powerful metaphor for human self-sabotage and destruction. A brilliantly crafted insight into the dark side of the human condition.

Praise for Mark's Work

"Without doubt, working with Mark was the turning point in my career."
Rory Best, Ulster, Ireland, British and Irish Lions

"I can say, without hesitation, that Mark Elliott is the best sport psychologist I have encountered."
Paul Brady, World Number 1 Handball Player

"I have a lot to thank Mark for."
Tommy Bowe, Ulster, Ireland, British and Irish Lions

"Mark has proven himself to be one of the top men in his field."
Martin McElkennon, Elite Trainer and Coach, Gaelic Football

"Mark is both a true expert in his field and a really good bloke."
Simon Danielli, formerly of Ulster and Scotland

Contents

Foreword

I first called Mark in September 2004, when playing on the European Challenge Tour. I had turned professional in 2002, following a successful amateur career, and had similar expectations for my professional life. Things hadn't worked out as I'd anticipated, and I was becoming frustrated with the game, even contemplating quitting. I had become fixated on my results and was extremely self-critical, viewing life in terms of golf scores.

Mark helped me to examine how I thought and behaved on and off the course. He helped me recognise that my poor mental habits were destroying my game and were actually preventing me becoming successful. With Mark's help I started work on training my mind and I won my first professional title, the BA-CA Golf Open in Austria, a short time later. Whilst adopting a more holistic approach to life and golf, my career has definitely improved and I won my 5th European Tour title earlier this year.

I therefore encourage you to read what Mark has to say and to follow his advice to improve your own mental game.

Best wishes.

Michael Hoey

December, 2013

www.mikehoeygolf.com

Introduction

In 2011 my first book was published. *Facing Frankenstein - Defeat Your True Opponent in Sport* was very well-received and became a bestseller. I've been thrilled by the positive response, and particularly pleased that athletes and coaches alike have successfully incorporated the book's teachings into their training and preparation for competition.

Since then, my sport psychology practice has expanded extensively, as performers from many different sports right across the world have contacted me for help. I have been running workshops and seminars almost constantly and giving impromptu talks on mental toughness in all sorts of unusual settings, including airport lounges and restaurants. There's a thirst for mental game knowledge of the like I've never experienced before. And it's great, because it means that people are waking up to the need to find a better way.

Moreover, many sports performers and coaches have been asking me to summarise my insight into the minds of world-class athletes into a kitbag-sized book. A book of mental toughness secrets!

And here it is - *Secrets of the Mentally Tough Athlete*. It's really good to see you here, as it tells me you're an ambitious athlete, one of the countless performers who have had enough of making-do and who now thirst for knowledge and change. You clearly want to improve your mental game and to perform with freedom and flow, excellence and enjoyment. Well, I'm delighted to tell you that you've definitely come to the right place, as this book will guide *you* to a *world-class* mental game. Yes, *you*. Yes, *world-class*.

And why not? After all, mental toughness and sporting greatness are not born, but made. They emerge from the chrysalis of deliberate action and quality effort. And you are just as capable as anyone else of doing the work. The simple truth is that those at the top of their sport made a decision to develop themselves to the maximum. They set about training both body *and* mind in a planned and purposeful way, making certain that no stone was left unturned, no neuron left untuned.

The best players on the planet take the mental game very seriously, knowing that it's often the one aspect of their training and performance that makes the difference between winning and losing. Recognising that their true opponent in sport lies within themselves, they work hard at building up their reserves of psychological skills to keep this inner saboteur at bay. At the end of the day, elite athletes are those who are best at managing themselves. They learn how to become mentally tough, not so much because sport exists, but because *they* exist. They have learned to reverse the self-sabotaging behaviour that afflicts most humans. So, when all is said and done, sport psychology is really about the psychology of being human in a world that insists we see ourselves as ordinary little creatures incapable of greatness. Now, before we go on, I want to set out the five key principles that lie beneath each and every strategy in this book:

1) Mental interference is self-created.
2) Peak performance is your natural state.
3) Interference, such as doubt, fear and distraction keeps you at arm's length from delivering high level displays on a consistent basis.
4) Mental toughness eliminates inner interference, allowing you to perform at your peak, as a matter of course.
5) Mental toughness is not a genetic gift, but something that can be developed.

Of course, the sixty secrets in this book shouldn't really be secrets at all. It shouldn't sound as though I'm some sort of Robert Langdon character, who has cracked a type of mental game Da Vinci Code, and who now brings to an awaiting world a long-buried scroll of tantalising secrets. Yet there's a part of me feels that what I'm providing in this book isn't that far removed from this scenario at all!

You see, on many occasions throughout my two decades in the field, I have been astonished by the lack of detailed inner game knowledge out there in the world of sport. Irrespective of the sport from which they come, the vast majority of athletes and coaches I've met and worked with have been unaware of what mental toughness really is and how to acquire it. It's as if the knowledge has indeed been suppressed. But, let me assure you, this book holds nothing back.

With *Secrets of the Mentally Tough Athlete* you have a practical book packed with specific skills, techniques, strategies and routines that are used by world-class athletes to become mentally tough. Each secret is not only presented in a user-friendly and straightforward way, but also has proven its effectiveness in the crucible of elite sport. Used by the very best to be the very best, you have right now at your fingertips *60* effective techniques you can begin to use immediately and that, once learned, will significantly strengthen your mental game and vastly improve your sports performance.

This book is for *all* athletes, regardless of their sport and level of ability. Mental toughness training is not just for the elite. Think about it, the elite would never have become elite in the first place, had they not engaged in mental skill training *during* their journey to the top. And this in truth is the biggest secret of them all - mental toughness is a must-have for the ambitious athlete.

What's mentally demanding about your sport? What aspects of competing are stressful for you? Consider the *before, during* and *after* phases of competition; then grab a pen and paper and note down your responses.

Okay, what have you recorded? Have you included such things as: making errors; performing in front of a large crowd/the national coach/the television cameras/your family; taking a crucial penalty/putt/free throw; waiting in the warm-up area before your race begins; being the favourite to win a match; being sledged by an opponent; receiving poor decisions by match officials?

These examples are, no doubt, the types of scenarios you find stressful in your sport, that as far as you're concerned, create the mental challenge. But they do nothing of the sort! They do *not* cause anything to happen.

You see, we've all been brought up to believe that our stress and anxiety is *caused* by unfavourable external events. That it is done to us. But this belief is completely illusory and dangerously wrong. The truth is we do it to ourselves.

At the end of the day, any situation that crops up in your sport, or in your life for that matter, is emotion-neutral, until you start thinking about it. Therefore the source of your stresses, anxieties and distractions lie within you; not out on the pitch, course, court, rink, or track.

Let's look at an example.

A golfer tees his ball up at the 14th, a right dogleg Par 5 hole with a lake looming large at the turn. It's a tricky drive, one requiring sound course management and precision. After consulting his caddy, the golfer decides to cut the corner and launch his drive over the water. It's risky, but if he pulls it off, the reward is good.

But the ball lands just short of the fairway and splashes into the lake.

What now for our guy?

Well, our golfer curses his idiocy for not being more cautious by playing the percentage shot instead. He calls himself all sorts of disparaging names for not laying up with an iron and, bizarrely, blames this error for the anxiety, irritation and frustration he's now beginning to experience. "Stupid ball", he remarks, before going on to make a complete hash of his next shot, his third. He ends up with a triple-bogey at the hole. For the remaining four holes, he continues to beat himself up and to blame the mistake for his agitation and poor showing over the closing holes.

So, this golfer blames his sport for causing his toxic emotional state and distraction. He's convinced that had the ball travelled a few more feet, away from the wet stuff, all would have been well with his world and perhaps he'd have gained a top ten finish.

Nonsense. The truth is he'd fallen prey to the 'Sport Illusion'. He believed that his emotional tailspin had been caused by golf itself. It never occurred to him to look inwards for answers. Instead, he became increasingly angry at how cruel golf was as a sport, and how it could transform an otherwise intelligent and calm person into a raging maniac! But he had turned himself into one and, in doing so, ruined his own round.

In this example, you can see where the psychological demand really resides when it comes to sport. It's within the athlete himself. Remember, the golf ball didn't know it was in the lake, in the same way that a rugby or tennis ball doesn't realise it has just skimmed past an upright or landed outside the tramlines. These are simply neutral incidents awaiting an interpretation. And it's the interpretation that colours in the emotional reaction. With our golfer using very dark colours!

Although unaware of it at the time, the golfer actually had an alternative response available to him after he'd landed the ball in the water. He could have remained positive, fought the urge to beat himself up, and talked to himself in a self-supportive way. A bit of perspective would've been useful too. His next shot could have been viewed as an opportunity to demonstrate his powers of recovery, and still make par. A 'still-all-to-play-for' mentality was an option the player didn't know he had.

The secret you're discovering here is hugely important and should form the foundation for all of your mental game work. You will not attain world-class mental toughness if you continue to believe that your sport causes you to feel anxious, angry, frustrated, dejected and so forth. Yes, your sport can lead to physical bruises, cuts and injuries but, no, it cannot cause a psychological meltdown. You do that bit yourself.

The world's best athletes have come to recognise the subtle truth contained within this secret, and live by it daily. They know that *playing sport is not mentally demanding. Rather they are*. Knowing this secret sparks their motivation to become mentally tough.

But there's more to know here, and it's a little bit sinister.

It's a sobering truth, but you, and all other athletes (well, all of us really) need to be mentally tough because of the single biggest flaw in the human condition. A highly destructive habit, learned from an early age, this flaw is the number one reason why so few of us are truly happy and successful in life. In fact, you've just witnessed it in action with our golfer. Its influence lay behind his ability to get in his own way and to destroy his performance. And I must tell you, it's also the reason why you too become your own worst enemy.

I call this self-sabotaging tendency, the *Frankenstein Factor*, and while the world's best may not refer to it in this way, I can assure you, they know all about it. And so must you.

I feel another secret coming on...

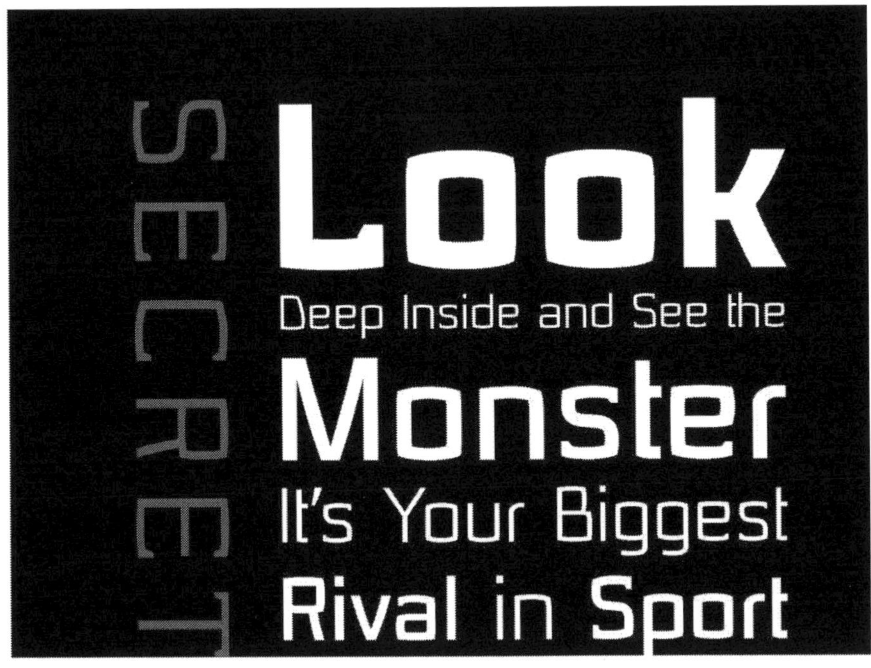

SECRET
Look
Deep Inside and See the
Monster
It's Your Biggest
Rival in Sport

In Secret 1 you discovered an amazing truth - that it's not sport, but athletes themselves who create the mental demand. In this section, you will learn how and why they do it.

Have you ever felt that your mind runs you, and not the other way round? That something lurks in your mind ready to ambush you during those critical moments before, during and after competition? For instance:

02

- You see how confident your opponent looks, and *it* strikes.
- You make a mistake, and *it* pounces.
- You recall a previous poor performance against today's opponents and *it* attacks.

- You place the ball on the penalty spot, and *it* swoops.

I'm pretty sure that these scenarios sound familiar to you. But what is the 'it'? What's the something inside your mind stealing your concentration, heightening your anxiety and planting seeds of doubt at the very time you really need to be focused, calm and confident? Why does it often feel as though another part of you is intent on wrestling peak performance and victory out of your very grasp?

If this all sounds a bit too familiar be reassured, you are not alone in this regard. The overwhelming majority of us experience such moments at key times in our lives, particularly in performance situations, where the spotlight of public scrutiny falls upon us. Our tendency to get in our own way, especially when other people are watching and judging, is something we have *learned* to do from a really young age, and become incredibly good at. And it's a process I have named the *Frankenstein Factor*, for reasons that will become clear.

I'm sure you'll agree that, as children, we were generally content, relaxed and comfortable in our own skin. We were highly imaginative and creative and seemed to just get on with things. We lived in the present without a care in the world. Mental interference (the bane of our existence, and something this book will help you eradicate) was a yet-to-be-created, self-imposed obstacle to a rewarding and successful life.

So what happened to turn us from happy and productive kids into success-starved self-saboteurs? Well, *society* 'happened' to us, that's what. By attending school we handed our brain over to other people, people whose agenda was to create left-brain-trained individuals for a left-brain world. The left side of the brain is concerned with such things as: language, thinking and analysing; logic and detail; the past and the future; and, being disconnected from the environment.

However, the right hemisphere has largely been overlooked by the education system. This means that the seat of our imagination and creativity has been disregarded. That the part of the brain concerned with 'the present', and which allows us to be at-one with an activity, has been underutilised. And you'll know that 'being at-one with an activity' is the very state an athlete wants to reach during his performance. In sporting circles it's called *the zone*, the quiet, in-the-moment place that allows an athlete's performance to flow and reach its peak.

So, there you have it. Our schooling has turned us into thinkers and analysers, clones of everyone else, who jump backwards and forwards between the past and the future, and who seldom live in the 'here-and-now'. Our minds have morphed into very noisy and cluttered places, with mental chattering an incessant feature of our daily lives.

All of this would be okay, of course, if our musings were constructive, positive and self-supporting. But this is often not the case. You see, while school taught us *how to think*, society has told us *what to think*. And let's just say the messages haven't exactly been enriching - in fact, they're often the very opposite.

Dispatched by parents, peers, teachers, politicians, clergy and the media, the messages we've received throughout our lives have been very negative and rigid; with danger, deference, inadequacy and restriction trending at any one moment. These dreadfully unhelpful messages have been lapped up by our well-trained and highly receptive left brains and have shaped how we think about ourselves, other people and our place in the world around us.

Our transformation from cheerful and confident children into skilled self-saboteurs means that each and every one of us has developed a highly destructive collection, or body, of mental habits. These viciously self-limiting beliefs and behaviours form what I call the *Mental Monster*.

Just as Mary Shelley's fictional Dr. Frankenstein cobbled together a physical creature that destroyed his world, so we have stitched together a host of negative beliefs, thoughts, messages and memories into our very own mental monster which wrecks our world, from the inside out.

While you can of course depict your inner opponent in whatever way you wish (you don't have to keep with the monster analogy) it nevertheless remains the case that your key opponent is you, and that you must do something about it. The greatest athletes in the world know that the 'it' that pounces at those crucial moments in competition, is that part of them created by the Frankenstein Factor and which is intent on getting in the way.

They realise that their main obstacle to success lies within, and that the only way to beat their inner foe is to become mentally tough. And they do - by adopting the philosophies, and carrying out the strategies, techniques and routines contained in this book.

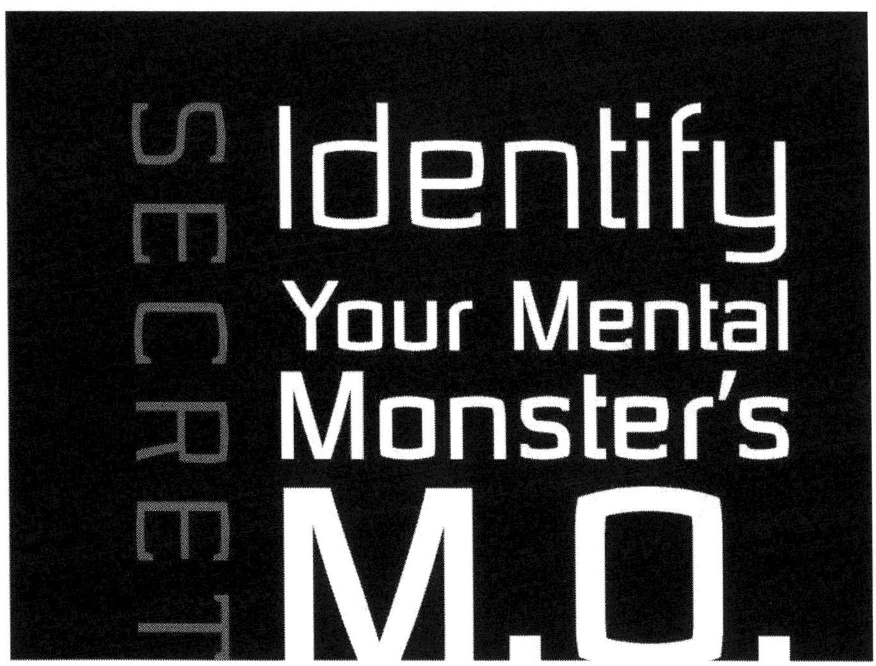
SECRET
Identify
Your Mental
Monster's
M.O.

03

The first step in overcoming your mental monster is to identify its motives, intentions and tactics - its modus operandi (M.O.). Only then can you ever begin to defeat it.

Monster's Motivation

This is a surprising one. The monster's aim is to protect your ego at all costs, and therefore it thinks it's doing you a favour. Created by you as a response to the indoctrination process (the Frankenstein Factor) the monster is, in effect, a massive defence mechanism against emotional pain. Where our cave-dwelling ancestors feared being injured or eaten by an animal, we fear attacks on our ego. Your mental monster, then, is motivated to protect your ego from the big cats of the modern age

- public failure, humiliation, disapproval, guilt and disgrace.

So, you have a duel in your crown - a contest between your true self (the one you were born with) and your artificial self (your mental monster). The former is motivated to be the best it can be; the latter, determined to avoid failure, embarrassment, derision and shame.

The really terrific news though, is that mental toughness returns you to your true self, and places you on the pathway to greatness.

Monster's Objective

Your mental monster's goal is to destroy your ambition from the inside. Personal advancement is far too risky a venture and your monster will have none of it. It cannot have you performing under the spotlight of public scrutiny, thereby courting the potential for failure and ridicule. As a result, it will do all it can to persuade you to make-do and to stop all that pie-in-the-sky dreaming about being a top athlete.

Its ultimate purpose is to keep you imprisoned in the narrowest of comfort zones, without you knowing it's even happening. After all, the greatest form of suppression is the type where the suppressed think they're free.

So, by infiltrating your thoughts, emotional state, and behaviour, your monster controls you; but you think you do. Clever, eh?

This is why most people can go through their entire lives without having an original thought or idea, and never reaching their true potential. Your mental monster is a devious opponent and one you must fight back against.

Monster's Tactics

Any saboteur worth its salt will attack where it can exert maximum mischief and impairment; and so it is with your mental monster. To keep you 'safe' from attacks on your ego, it engineers a hostile takeover of your brain's fantastic systems to keep you in the smallest of comfort zones. This process is so gradual that you may not realise you're trapped; it'll feel normal, as all well-engrained habits do.

Your mental monster uses its wily ways to change the culture of your mental environment. You'll know this is happening when you begin to focus much more on avoiding failure and humiliation, than on pursuing success and satisfaction. This negative and risk-averse shift in your intention will shape everything that you do. Your thoughts will be about threats, not opportunities; about anxiety and not excitement; and about not losing rather than winning.

Your inner monster will wreak havoc across your mind, hijacking your brain's systems to seize control over your motivation, thoughts, beliefs, concentration, emotions and imagination. By capturing these six key functions, it captures YOU. It places you in the prison without bars - FEAR - and stops you from discovering who you really are and that you were born with everything you ever needed to attain greatness in your sport, and fulfilment in your life.

Carry out a living autopsy on your mental monster and you'll find some of these horrid habits:

- Seeking validation and approval from other people.
- Fear of being embarrassed and ridiculed.
- Problems coping with change and uncertainty.
- Fear of failure/Perfectionism.
- Difficulty accepting *what is* - distracted instead by *what should have been.*
- Dwelling on mistakes.
- Difficulty living and performing in the present moment.

- Repeatedly agitated by the past and worried about the future.
- Easily frustrated and angered.

Incidentally, to illustrate just how crafty your mental monster really is, consider this. Your 'self-created inner enemy' is both the reason why you need to develop your mental game, *and* the reason why you've avoided doing so! This meddler of the mind has placed you, all of us, in an emotional double bind. It causes our stress and angst and then has the gall to alert us to the societal view that asking for help, particularly on psychological issues, is a sign of weakness, a flaw in our character. This explains why athletes tend to consult sport psychologists only when they have to; when they have hit some sort of personal rock bottom.

Monster's Capability

Let me put this as clearly as possible: Your mental monster has the capacity to DESTROY your sports career.

But you can defeat it by choosing to become mentally tough.

And, YES, it is a choice.

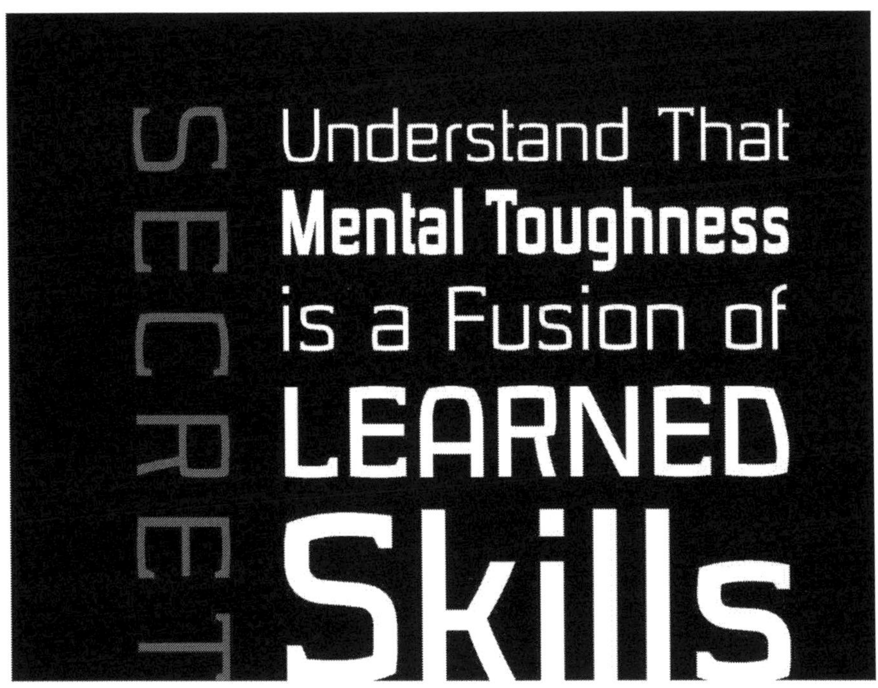

SECRET
Understand That
Mental Toughness
is a Fusion of
LEARNED
Skills

04

It's time to fight back against your mental monster, a battle that'll determine whether or not you become world-class in your sport. It is, of course, a battle that champions fight and win. And now it's your turn.

There's no magic to becoming mentally tough. As with all aspects of sports preparation, it requires time, patience, and above all, quality practice. When we see top performers in full flow, doing amazing things, it can appear as if they have an extra dollop of DNA that makes them superhuman. That sets them apart from the rest of us. But this is another illusion.

The difference is neither mysterious nor genetic. Instead, these high achievers *self-*

select and *decide* to develop their minds. They aspire to be total performers, 4D exponents of their craft. They realise that being proficient in the technical, physical and tactical dimensions is simply insufficient as these three outer game elements of sports preparation and performance can be trumped by a poor inner game. So, they face up to their mental monster by *learning* skills that fuse into the attribute we call *mental toughness*.

Athletes can give themselves a considerable competitive advantage by engaging in psychological skills training to defeat their mental monster.

As the majority of sports performers either don't know how to train their brain, or can't be bothered doing so, an athlete who does become mentally tough will start to stand out from the crowded middle ground of mediocrity. And when you think about it, that's what the world's best ultimately do - stand out from the crowd.

A really good way to think about the mental monster and mental toughness is to see them as opposites. The monster is a fusion of *destructive* mental habits, while mental toughness is a fusion of *constructive* mental habits. Where one is a *poor* mental game, the other is a *great* one.

The following Table provides a stark illustration of how they differ.

The Monster-Munched Athlete is...	The Tough Minded Athlete is...
Driven to attain external rewards	Motivated from within
Self-conscious and shallow	Self-assured and self-effacing
A slave to his unhelpful mental chatter	In control of his thoughts

Distracted by irrelevancies	Focused on the process of achievement
A hostage to negative imagery	In control of his imagination
Easily hijacked by his nervous system	The master of his emotions

Elite athletes know which type of mental game they want, and work hard to achieve it. They are acutely aware that mental toughness is the only weapon that can:

- Eliminate the interference spewed out by their inner saboteur.
- Clear the path to peak performance on a regular basis.

The gateways to mental toughness are found within your brain's incredible systems. However, due to the Frankenstein Factor, your mental monster gate-crashed your brain and twisted your perception of yourself, other people, and the world around you.

As explained in the last secret, it took control of your motivation, self-belief, interpretive ability, concentration, imagination, and emotional state. And, therefore, of you and your life; sporting or otherwise.

You'll not be surprised to learn that becoming mentally tough involves the gradual process of taking back full control of these very same brain systems. To do this, you need to participate in a structured programme of mental skills training that will target these six systems and return them to their natural state: that is, working for and not against you.

Basically, mental toughness is about learning skills that, once acquired, will enable you to:

- Become self-motivated to engage in quality training, to persist in the face of setbacks, and to attain significant improvements in performance.
- Shape your own positive reality through thinking and imaging in really helpful ways.
- Silence your mind while preserving an in-the-moment focus during performance.
- Feel ready for whatever competition throws at you.
- Reach your Personal Ideal Performance State (PIPS) time after time.
- Believe in yourself like never before.

It's important to remember that mental toughness is a blend of skills and not a single entity. What's more, as these skills are learnable, you have the opportunity to develop a wonderful inner game.

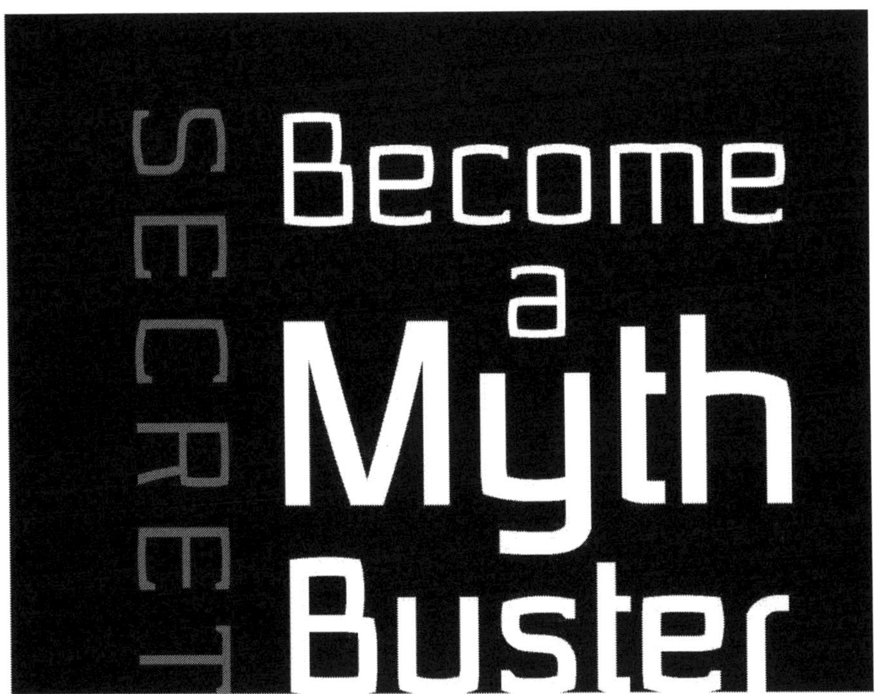
SECRET
Become
a
Myth
Buster

05

The overwhelming majority of us are influenced and duped by the following three myths:

- The Illusion of Separateness.
- The Illusion of Time.
- The Illusion of Self-Importance.

If you believe these illusions, you place a restriction on your capacity to deliver high level sports performances on a consistent basis and to ever attain world-class status.

You've no chance. These three fables are monster fodder. Why? Because they limit your perception of what is possible.

Myth of Separateness

The *Illusion of Separateness* perpetuates the notion that we are apart from the world around us, and therefore encourages us to look outside of ourselves for happiness and fulfilment. It's as if the environment itself can provide the psychological nutrients for a satisfying and contented life. So we go foraging for such things as money, material possessions, celebrity life, approval and status. This is a soulless existence and will never sustain us over the longer term. The source of enduring success, in sport and life, lies *within* us.

Also, the Illusion of Separateness has duped us into believing that unfavourable external events *cause* our stress, frustration, anger, distraction and so on. As one of the human race's most limiting beliefs, this illusion has fooled millions-upon-millions of athletes into believing that sport itself is psychologically demanding. That it's the penalty miss, the shanked drive, or the umpire's harsh decision that causes all sorts of unsettling feelings. But it's simply not the case. It's the footballer, golfer and tennis player themselves who cause their own interference.

It's vital to recognise your own role in shaping your emotional state, and that you're *not* a passive victim of life's 'slings and arrows'. You are *not* a powerless character in some twisted Playstation game, and you're not going to be tricked by this illusion any more. Right? After all, in the language of gaming, you possess an unmatchable control, one that can never be replicated by the Sonys of this world - the human brain. You alone have the intellectual capacity to interpret an unfavourable situation in a more favourable way.

Myth of Time

Although clocks exist, time doesn't. The only moment that ever exists is NOW, and nothing else. While I agree that without our calendars, diaries and watches life would be extremely chaotic, the notion of time being an active and organic thing has tricked us into wasting considerable amounts of energy scuttling between two illusory places - the past and the future. Yet, when we mentally travel to these 'places' we do so in the present. And if, in the present, we are in the middle of competition, then valuable focus has been squandered.

Myth of Self-Importance

To believe that the world revolves around us, and that we are central to other people's lives, is a delusion of catastrophic proportions. We can spend a lifetime obsessed with what other people are thinking about us, when the truth is they're not that interested in us at all!

As with the myth of separateness, this illusion ties you into the external world - in this case to other people. Those who fall for this myth, end up with a host of hang-ups and distractions. Their sense of self-worth is handed over to (perceived) public opinion and they end up fretting about their reputation. They dread being derided and having their overblown ego pierced. In fact, they are prone to bouts of jealousy and resentment, as they witness their peers advancing their lot in life. This is not only an unpleasant way to be, but also forms a significant barrier to the chances of attaining real success.

Mentally tough athletes are not sheep: they think for themselves

Most of us have never been told that these three beliefs are actually myths, and self-limiting ones at that. We accept these views unquestioningly and then wonder why our lives are so stressful and our goals remain unmet. This is how it is for the vast majority of the population.

But there are those who seek the truth about who they are, what is possible, and how to attain greatness. These open-minded individuals are the top performers and achievers in our world today. They actively challenge their thinking and interpretative style and refuse to be vacuous receptacles of hand-me-down beliefs, particularly when the beliefs place them in a tiny box of possibility.

Before they became world-beaters, elite athletes were myth-busters. They confronted the myths of separateness, time and specialness and started to consider the world around them, and their place within it, in a healthier and more self-sufficient way.

Now it's over to you. You can either be an unquestioning sheep and fool yourself that greatness is an impossible goal, as the bulk of the world's flock do, or you can engage your intellect and begin to think for yourself and make things happen.

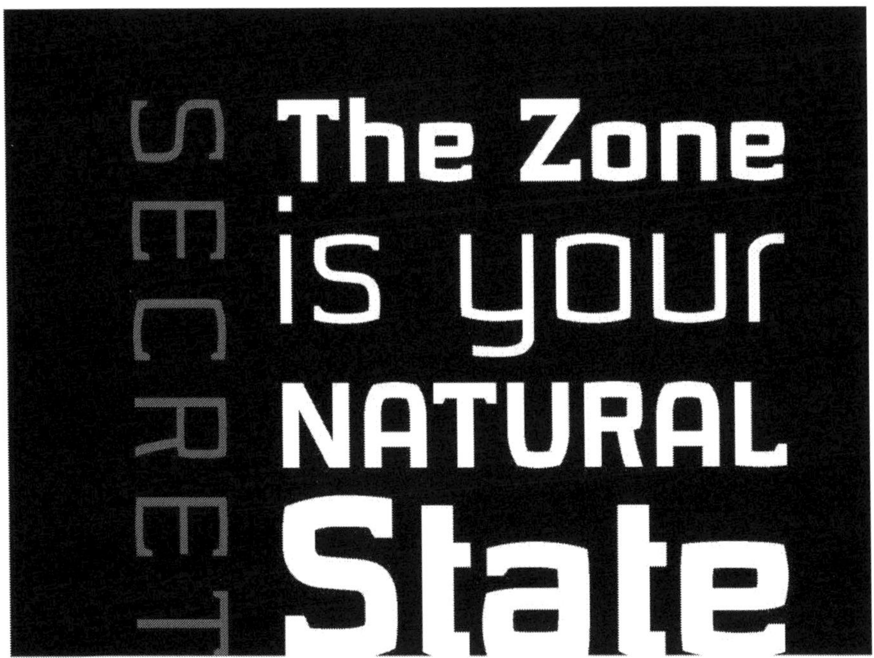

'The Zone' is the sporting Nirvana inhabited by the best athletes in world sport. It is the unforced and graceful state where brain, body and environment become one, and when athletes perform at their peak, enjoying every moment of the experience. It is common for zoned-in performers to report that they:

- Felt calm and confident throughout their performance.
- Were totally focused in the here-and-now.
- Performed with ease.
- Had great fun.

They will also speak of performing 'out of their minds'- that their performances were beyond the reach of mental interference. Everything was quiet. Everything just flowed in harmony. I'm sure you'd be over the moon to be able to perform with such ease, enjoyment and excellence on a regular basis. It'd be just wonderful wouldn't it? Well, here's something amazing for you, an exciting secret that should motivate you to start training your brain at once: THE ZONE IS YOUR NATURAL STATE!

Yes, it really is!

It's how we were all meant to be - living and performing more fully in the present.

But, sadly, due to the ways in which we've been educated and socialised, our mental focus has been shifted too firmly into the left brain, whose function is largely about analysis, detail and separateness.

Our focus has been funnelled as far away from the zone as possible; meaning that reaching peak performance has become the exception, rather than the rule for many of us: a pleasant surprise, rather than a matter of course.

As a result, every athlete who is serious about making the grade has to battle back with all of his might. And the fight is against the incredibly noisy, ego-infested, past and future obsessed left brain, which has become the home of the modern human's mind.

As I stress at each one of my seminars, workshops and athlete consultations, *the greatest performers on the planet plot their course to success.*

It is a meticulously designed journey that involves physical and psychological preparation, with mental toughness acting as a type of 'snowplough' that clears a pathway through the white noise of mental interference and on through to the zone. Accordingly, the mind quietens, focus becomes absolute, and skills are unleashed with excellence in the present, until the job is done.

By performing out of their minds, both metaphorically and literally, the world's top athletes have in effect shifted their focus from left brain intrusion to right brain artistry.

The best athletes on the planet make the 'peak performance formula' work for them - and so must you. The formula is:

Peak Performance = Capability *minus* **interference** (or, PP=C-i)

By 'Capability', I am describing the part of your performance that we can all see - your technique, physical strength, fitness and endurance.

In other words, your OUTER game.

However, your capability, your 'C', is not a constant, as it can be profoundly influenced by your INNER game; the game we can't see. And this is where the formula comes into its own. If the Frankenstein Factor didn't exist, and we didn't learn to get in our own way, then the formula would simply be PP=C. So, aside from injury or earthquakes, your potential to deliver a high level performance would be the sole product of your physical and technical ability. In fact, your impressive performances in practice would transfer seamlessly to the competitive setting.

Oh, how good would this be?!!!!

Yes, it would be great, but things are what they are. We have been socialised to sabotage our own efforts and therefore the peak performance formula has to take account of the mental side of things. Your preparation and performance can be polluted by such mental interference as doubt, lethargy, nervousness, fear of failure, and distraction. These fall within the ambit of the **'i'** in the formula.

So, what does the ambitious athlete do? Well, he must train both his mind and body to ensure that he keeps raising his 'C' and lowering his **'i'**. In doing this, he will optimise his efforts in competition. He will deliver peak performances on an ongoing basis.

Incidentally, when you look at the formula you can also see why the highly capable sports performer can bomb-out in competition, and often to opponents who are, 'on paper', much less technically competent.

To illustrate what I mean by this, let's enter the world of elite junior tennis, a competitive world if ever there was one, and discover how the less talented Morgan tends to beat his more talented rival Zach. In fact, out of their last ten meetings, Morgan has won eight.

Right, first up we have 13 year-old Zach, an extremely capable tennis player, whose outer game, 'C', is very high (let's rate it at a 9/10). Good start. However, as his inner game is really weak, and he experiences a high degree of mental interference, his **'i'** comes in at 6/10. Place these figures into the formula and you can see at an instant how Zach's inadequate mental game rips up his 'on paper' superior capability, leaving his overall performance floundering at a disappointing **3**. This is well below his potential and extremely frustrating for both Zach and his coach.

Morgan's a different kettle of fish, however. Here we have another 13 year-old player, but one who squeezes every last drop out of his relatively limited capability by employing psychological techniques that keep his **'i'** very low. So, although Morgan's 'C' is assessed as 6 out of 10 (compared to Zach's 9), he has little in the way of mental interference, thanks to his robust inner game. Consequently his **'i'** is well down the scale, coming in at a very respectable 2. Quickly doing the maths tells us that Morgan's outright performance in his latest battle with Zach is a **4**. Just enough to outshine his higher-ranked opponent. In this real life example, Morgan has exploited an important performance secret - *sport is played between the ears, and not on paper*.

Olympic Gold Medallist, Amy Williams, says:

> *"You can have someone who's got massive talent, but if they don't have the attitude and that drive to succeed then they won't make it. Equally, someone who has maybe got a bit less talent but has got all the rest, they'll make it."* - BBC Sport.

Mark Selby, one of the world's best snooker players, is also certain that the **'i'** within the peak performance formula is *the* most important factor of all at the elite level:

> *"The mental side of it is probably 90% of the game. There are hundreds of players who can make century breaks and 147s, but*

not everyone seems to produce at the top level and that is down to the mental state." - BBC Sport.

When the world's best tell you these things, I believe you should listen. Start to consider your own **'i'** factor and build up a profile of its current status. For all you know, it may well be devouring your capability in big bites.

SECRET
Book Yourself in
for a
Mental
Game
Scan

To develop mental toughness, you need to get things right at the very start of the learning process. You need to know where:

- You're headed (i.e. what mental toughness 'looks like').
- Your mental game is right now.

If you do not prepare for your journey in this detailed way, then it's highly likely that your motivation to improve your inner game will evaporate in the heat of frustration and stagnation.

Although these are obvious starting points to achieving any goal in life, it is surprising to discover that many athletes fail to carry out such assessments with any degree of sophistication and commitment. Instead, there is a tendency towards haphazardness, and a feeling that such detailed introspection is unnecessary. These performers seldom make it big.

Predictably, top athletes are incredibly excited by this part of the improvement process and prepare in a structured way for the road ahead. And so should you, if you want to make massive progress in your mental game.

Mental Game Scan

As you discovered earlier in the book, mental toughness is an umbrella term for a range of psychological characteristics that can be learned. From my twenty-two years working with some of the world's best performers, I've been able to distil these features into six mental game areas: internal motivation; strong self-belief; constructive thinking; appropriate focus; imagery control; and, emotional control.

These pillars of mental toughness are set out below, in the form of what a 10 out of 10 rating would look like for each desirable quality. You see, I want you to rate your mental game against each of these six descriptions, using a 0-10 scale. You will only apply a rating of '0' if you believe you are completely deficient in any of the mental game areas.

1) Motivation

- You are highly motivated to succeed, moved to do so out of an inner desire to be the best you can be.
- You enjoy pursuing excellence in your sport as you are working towards personal goals.
- You are extremely hungry to succeed: nothing will stand in your way.

- You persevere in the face of misfortune, remaining positive, confident and focused.
- You possess a high tolerance for frustration and see change as a challenge, rather than a threat.
- Your motivational power is not plugged-in to the external grid of money, public acclaim and fame. Instead, it is internally generated by the satisfaction you draw from making progress and performing well in your sport.
- Your ego does not get in the way when it comes to seeking out expert guidance.

Your Rating: /10

2) **Self-Belief**

- You have a solid sense of self-worth.
- You accept who you are and value your place in the world.
- You are comfortable in your own skin and are not consumed by what others think of you.
- You live *your* life, no-one else's. Born an original, you refuse to die a copy.
- You are highly confident in your ability to achieve your goals.
- Your confidence is based on evidence, not built on sand.
- You are unassuming and therefore have no desire to tell people how great you are.

Your Rating: /10

3) **Constructive Thinking**

- You know that your reality is the product of how you think about things.
- You have outstanding thinking skills.
- You are adept at identifying, challenging and changing unhelpful thoughts.

- Your ability to interpret situations constructively enables you to control your emotions, increase your confidence, ignite your motivation and sharpen your focus.

Your Rating: /10

4) Focus

- You are able to concentrate fully on what matters right now.
- Your focus no longer runs pointless errands between the past and the future.
- You can adjust your focus effortlessly during performance.
- Your ability to compete moment-by-moment with a calm, non-judgemental mind ensures that your talent is not dumped in the mental wasteland of distraction.

Your Rating: /10

5) Imagery Control

- You are skilled in using imagery, finding it to be the most versatile of mental game tools.
- You use your mental *iPlayer* to access, again and again, your unmissable collection of excellent performances stored on mental tape. These memories and images are yours and ready at a moment's notice to be replayed in your mind.
- You use imagery to help you prepare for competition, manage critical moments during performance, and to review your efforts after competition.

Your Rating: /10

6) Emotional Control

- You have the passion to pursue excellence, and the composure to attain it.
- You realise that pressure is not 'out there' in the environment ready to pounce like some type of predator,

but instead is an internal affair, created by poor mental skills. This discovery has put you in the driving seat of emotional control.

- You know your PIPS - your Personal Ideal Performance State.
- You are your own emotional thermostat, able to adjust your arousal to the ideal level.
- You are always ready to perform, motivated and up for the challenge.
- You are a fearless competitor whose mantra is "Bring it on!"

Your Rating: /10

What you have achieved by rating your mental game across these six areas, is that you now have a yardstick against which you can gauge your progress as you set about applying the strategies and routines in this book. You now know how strong your mental game is, and what mental toughness is all about.

This groundwork is incredibly important. It provides you with a strong foundation on which to build the toughest of mental games. It also allows you to make specific plans based on specific knowledge, and gives you the chance to plot your course to success. And as you embark on this journey, remember to check your mental game at regular intervals, otherwise you'll lose sight of how you're getting on.

SECRET
Plot
the
Coordinates
for
Greatness

World-class athletes are route-finders who plot their course to greatness by converting their dreams into well thought-out goals. They achieve this by making sure their goals meet the criteria laid down by the 'PUMAA test'. PUMAA is an acronym I use to encapsulate the five essential elements of effective goals. These are: **P**recise, **U**nderstood, **M**ine, **A**chievable and **A**djustable.

09

If you really want to set yourself on the pathway to excellence, then look no further than the PUMAA goal setting system, as it encourages you to:

1. Know precisely what it is you want to achieve, and the specific actions you

will take to improve the targeted skill, and by when.

2. Be in no doubt about what it is you have to do and the actual training methods you will use.
3. Be certain that the dream you're pursuing is *your* dream; that it's not for your coach, nor your parents, and definitely not to get back at some naysayer from your past. It is about being able to truthfully declare that: "My goals are just that - MINE. They inspire *me*."
4. Know that, within reason, your goals are under your control to achieve.
5. Have the wisdom to allow for the unexpected, such as illness and injury, leaving wiggle room for adjustments to your achievement plan.

It's important to tell you that all too often athletes neglect the mental side, only setting goals for developing their technical skills and physical fitness. But the great ones stay ahead of everyone else by approaching their inner game development as they do the other elements of their sport. They profile their psychological skills and set goals to sharpen them. In doing so, they learn how to think, feel, imagine and act in ways that allow their talent to shine through unimpeded by mental interference.

So, when plotting your course to success, remember to set PUMAA goals for strengthening your mental skills.

SECRET
Set Your
Motivational
Compass
to
Internal

10

Are you just a patchwork quilt of other people's expectations, needs and opinions? Or are you instead a self-sufficient human unit, driven from within to be everything you can be?

Well, chances are you're somewhere in-between. Most of us are like this, but aren't aware of it; which is the scary bit. It's alarming because we'd like to think that all of our choices are freely made. But due to how we have been socialised, many of us fail to see the join between the subliminal messages we receive from society and our own true intentions. I always start off my sessions with athletes by asking them why they're competing in their sport. I want to know who or what they're doing it all for. Those 6am training runs, the airports, the delayed flights, the hotel rooms, the media onslaught, the defeats, the injuries, the family left at home, the problems maintaining relationships...

Why?

World class sports performers are almost offended by this enquiry, puzzled by its relevance. Of course they're doing it for themselves, they'll say. If further proof was needed, these top athletes are also the ones who pass what I call the *Solo Hole-in-One Test*. And here it is:

> *You are on your own teeing off at a Par3 on your local golf course. You hit a beauty and in it goes for an ace. However, you realise that no-one was watching. What happens next? Do you feel devastated that the hole-in-one wasn't witnessed? Or are you just glad that you were there to see it?!*

The best athletes nail this test in an instant: *"Yeah, Mark, I'd just be glad I was there."* They wouldn't be irritated that no-one else was there to see their moment of success. They'd just feel a great sense of personal satisfaction.

Okay, you have a go.

Read over the scenario and note the thoughts and feelings that are stirred up by the narrative. Don't underestimate the power of this little test as it offers an indication of which direction your motivational compass is headed.

Now, if you'd be very disappointed that you were on your own at the time, then your motivational compass is largely directed to things *external* to you, and over which you have little or no control. However, if you would be happy that the hole-in-one had occurred at all, and that it was a pleasant moment in itself, without an audience, then rest assured, you are mostly *internally* driven and therefore in control. Just as the world's best are - they too take pleasure and satisfaction from a job well done. There is a spark inside of them that grows throughout the process of skill development and achievement.

Internal motivation generates an independence of thought and action. An athlete with an inner passion to improve is a performer in harmony with his goals. They are personal to him, he owns them, and he understands how they fit in to the big picture.

As he is accountable for goal-realisation, he will move Heaven and Earth to get the job done, and persevere longer than his rivals when times are tough. Because he really wants something, he will train in a purposeful way, and take satisfaction from progress made. Success will not be shouted about from the rooftops. Instead, it will be used as kindling for his inner spark.

No athlete can realise his ambition by feeding off such motivational foodstuffs as public approval, money and media attention. While some early success can emerge, the really ambitious performer needs to look deep inside for more enduring sustenance for the journey ahead. He needs to have the mental equivalent of a camel's hump, an internal store of incentives to help him carry on during the dry season; times when enthusiasm dips and progress stalls.

It's a sad state of affairs, but many of us are 'approval-seeking junkies'. We place our feelings of self-worth in the hands of our 'dealers' - other people. As having our egos boosted is a very addictive habit, it is important for you to reflect on the main source of your self-esteem and to gauge the extent to which it is intertwined with a need to please others and to gain their approval.

If you are an approval junkie, then you must take stock, because the inevitable is going to happen to you, sooner rather than later. Your sources will dry up, you'll not receive your fix, and you'll undergo motivational cold turkey. As a result, the quality of your training and your ability to deliver peak performances will be significantly compromised.

When you cease to be flavour of the month, and the media and public shift their attention to the new kid on the block, what is going to drive you on? What can you fall back on to generate your motivation to succeed? When your performances take a plunge and you can't buy a win, how will you keep going if the source of your motivation is in the hands of others? You know, when they aren't clapping anymore, or chanting your name, and your favourite sports journalist no longer calls?

What then?

The best cure is prevention and you can get working on this right away. You don't need to be revered, approved of, or admired. You need to build up an inner reservoir of motivation.

You need to turn your motivational compass to INTERNAL.

SECRET
Unnamed Law:
If It Happens,
It Must
Be Possible

There is a profound rule that elite athletes have followed since they first became eager to reach the top. It's obvious when you hear it, and incredibly motivating when you live by it, yet numerous athletes are oblivious to this awesome law. As a result, they miss out on shaping their mentality and firing up their motivation in an astonishingly powerful way.

11

When some of the athletes who watched Sir Roger Bannister break the (allegedly unbreakable) 'four minute mile' applied this law to their own circumstances, they started to think in new ways. They ripped off the shackles of limitation and fostered an 'I can' attitude. As a result, they too completed a mile in under four minutes and, in doing so, confirmed the reliability of a simple rule, one that's as dependable as any law of physics. And it is this: 'If It Happens, It Must Be Possible'.

Marcus Aurelius hinted at this law in his writings:

> *"If you find a thing difficult, consider whether it would be possible for any person to do it. Because anything that is humanly possible, that falls within human capabilities - you too can accomplish."*

Now if this law doesn't inspire you to approach your training in a deliberate and passionate way and to really believe that you can develop into an exceptional athlete, then very little else will. And if this is the case, then you should reassess your motives.

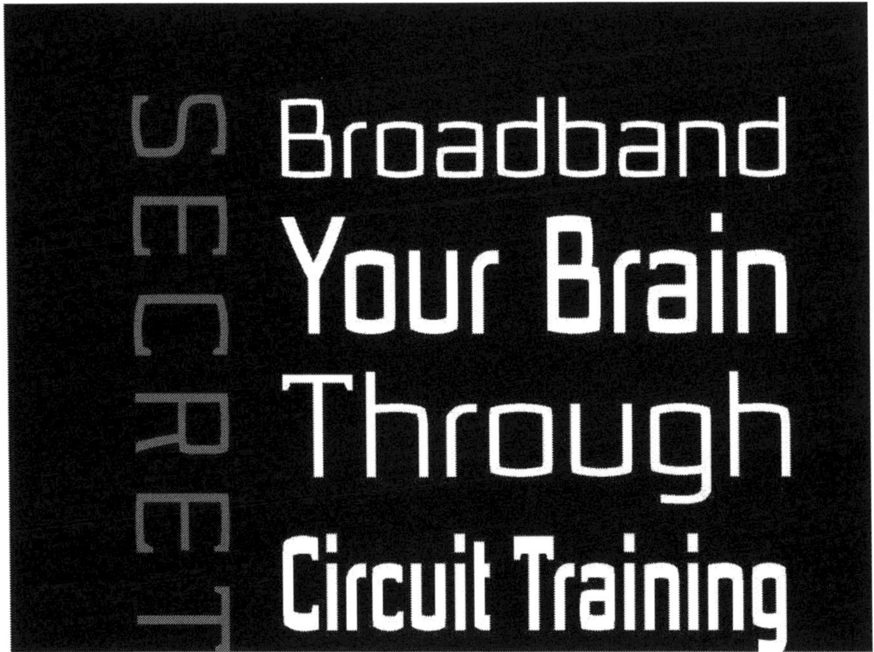
SECRET
Broadband
Your Brain
Through
Circuit Training

In his book, *The Talent Code*, Daniel Coyle describes how a training system called *deep practice* (also referred to as deliberate practice) causes REAL CHANGE to occur in the brain. Deep practice is a meticulous process of skill-stretching and sculpting that turns base potential into golden world-class ability. It is what elite performers engage in, while their less-skilled rivals remain wedded to their comfort zones.

12

When all is said and done, deep practice is about HOW you train and not simply about how often. Take golf, for instance. How many players spend their practice time, day-after-day, hitting hundreds of golf balls on the range, with only the final shot having any sense of purpose to it? An incalculable number, I would say. And why the last shot? Well, because the golfer wants to feel good before he returns to the locker room. As a result, he'll place greater focus on the last ball in the bucket and if it goes well, he may skip back to the clubhouse deceiving himself that "my practice went well today". Now, if ever there was an example of hollow and self-delusional practice, that's it right there.

Saying that you train every day is meaningless, unless you're adhering to certain principles and protocols. Namely, those advocated by deep practice.

Deep practice is a scrupulously planned approach to performance improvement where, in terms of sport, the ambitious athlete will repeatedly extend his abilities just beyond the existing level. For you, this means that bit-by-painstaking-bit you will shape your skills (including your mental skills) through a precise and systematic cycle of planning, doing, evaluating and refining. With guidance on hand from an expert coach, you will find out the correct way to execute a skill before then rehearsing it repeatedly, stretching it, rehearsing it again, and so on, until the objective is reached.

Unlike the golf example, above, a deep practice session is a goal-directed and honest pursuit, with every activity within it having a purpose. Nothing is wasted, as learning and progressing is the name of the game.

The truly exciting piece of news emanating from Coyle's work is that by engaging in deep practice you can upgrade your brain's neural circuitry! It can become like broadband in its wiring and messaging ability - and all thanks to a brain tissue called *myelin*.

Myelin is a neural insulator, a substance that wraps itself around nerve fibres in the brain in direct response to focused, repetitive practice of a skill, action or thought. It works by improving the strength, speed and accuracy of the particular neural pathway. As Coyle explains, "*The more we fire a particular circuit, the more myelin optimizes that circuit, and the stronger, faster, and more fluent our movements and thoughts become.*"

Crucially, however, myelin does not distinguish between constructive and destructive skill-development. It simply lags the neural circuit relevant to the repeatedly rehearsed skill; be it a technical or mental skill. It's the case, then, that due to the Frankenstein Factor many of us have unintentionally myelinated our brain circuits for such dreadfully unhelpful skills as: fearing failure and ridicule; dwelling on errors; beating ourselves up; remaining in our narrow comfort zones; distraction from the task-at-hand; and, toxic anxiety.

Yes, these are *skills,* and plenty of people are expert self-saboteurs. At the end of the day, your mental monster is simply a set of poor and obstructive mental skills that you have myelinated into your brain circuitry. Therefore, if you're serious about improving your inner game, you need to myelinate neural pathways for such mental toughness qualities as self-belief, productive thinking, imagery control, composure, error-management and effective focus.

What this means, is that by applying the principles of deep practice to your mental game development, you will, in due course, GROW your very own champion's mindset - literally!

And believe me, there is no greenhouse in existence capable of doing that!

SECRET 13: Make Friends with Failure

When you engage in deliberate practice, in continuously shaping and extending your skill-sets, then you're going to make errors. You are going to fail many times as you keep pushing your abilities beyond the comfort zone. That's just the way it is. Expecting anything other than this is foolhardy in the extreme.

The simple truth is that world-class performers not only expect to make mistakes, they also welcome them. Ambitious athletes are like ambitious students - they don't just keep revising the easy stuff. They enthusiastically take on new challenges, accepting that they will fall short at times in their pursuit of proficiency.

Successful sportspeople view errors as vital to their learning and development; not as threats to their ego.

They don't see mistakes as potholes on the road to excellence, but as cat's eyes guiding them out of the comfort zone and into the improvement zone.

Sport's 'also-rans' have extreme difficulty managing mistakes. Controlled by their mental monster, they beat themselves up, dread making further errors, become distracted, and underperform. In doing this, they sabotage their chances of ever making it big.

Many careers end this way.

So, if you want to excel in your sport, to become great at what you do, then you must make friends with failure. Or, as Thomas Watson the founder of IBM put it: "*If you want to succeed, double your failure rate.*"

SECRET
Follow
the
Discomfort

14

The vast majority of us recoil at the thought of stepping outside our comfort zone. Instead, we're inclined to cosy-up to the status quo, and remain within the narrow boundaries of a life half-lived.

A life of restriction, where risk is shunned, and fulfilment sabotaged.

It's the case that all growth is preceded by some form of discomfort and pain. That's a given; that's life. And it also goes a long way to explain why so few people attain success. While many of us dream about making it big in sport, business, music or education, the people who actually deliver on their dreams are those who have learned to withstand doubt and uneasiness. They persist in the face of adversity; they feel the fear and do it anyway. They are mentally tough.

However, many sports performers have great difficulty holding out when fear hits. Well to be fair, we all do. We all have an urge to back out and avoid the thing we fear, which is a totally reasonable reaction at one level, but extremely myopic at another. It's rational to want to avoid pain, particularly when faced with a genuine threat to our wellbeing and safety. But such evasion is a shortsighted tactic for an athlete whose fear is founded in the ego - where he fears failure, ridicule and embarrassment.

For the world's best athletes, playing safe is never a valid option, particularly on the back of mental discomfort. Instead, they exploit a wonderful secret - they run towards the discomfort, not away from it! They follow their unsettling feelings and learn through time that anxiety, apprehension and nervousness are just beacons on the road to excellence. Signs that tell them it's time to grow a little more; to move beyond their current comfort zone and to take on new challenges.

You see, your discomfort represents the boundary of your current comfort zone, be that around a specific skill set or social situation, and as such should be welcomed, not shunned. After all, it tells you that a particular area requires attention. This information is of massive importance and should be acted upon as soon as possible. But, as always, it's your choice. Abraham Maslow put it well when he said: "*You will either step forward into growth, or you will step back into safety.*"

SECRET 15 Ridicule Is Nothing to be scared of

I guess when you dress as a mixture of trendy Hussar and Dandy Highwayman, with what looks like a streak of tippex dissecting your face from cheekbone-to-cheekbone, worrying about being derided is just not on your radar. You see, Eighties icon, Adam Ant, the flamboyant lead singer of pop sensation Adam and the Ants, practiced what he preached. He refrained from worrying about what other people thought of him and even insisted, through his lyrics, that we should all follow his lead as really there was nothing to fear anyway. 'Ridicule Is Nothing to Be Scared Of' are his words, not mine, and come from the Ants' hit single *Prince Charming*.

Adam was clearly on to something. He realised

that the fear of ridicule was a major obstacle to people attaining success, and that the only way to overcome it was to push on regardless. In this way, we'd soon discover that the fear was groundless all along!

Wise counsel, indeed. Yet it has largely gone unheeded, as far too many of us continue to sacrifice our desire for self-improvement on the altar of 'people worry'.

People worry is the psychological equivalent of 'locked in syndrome', with an individual's true, limitless self, imprisoned behind all sorts of anxieties and fears, with the fear of ridicule the most powerful of the lot. This one fear alone can keep you away from discovering who you really are, and that you possess the potential to be whatever you want to be. If not challenged and confronted, this particular fear can end your career.

This would be really sad, for three main reasons:

1. You cannot control what people are going to think or say anyway - so you may as well just get on with things.
2. You can always choose not to be offended by anything you read or hear.
3. You aren't that important. Most people, who witness your poor performance, or big mistake, DON'T CARE. They just go home after the game and get on with *their* lives!

The secret, here, is that the fear of ridicule is much more potent than the ridicule itself. I guess most fears work this way. When the feared event does occur, we tend to cope much better than we thought we would. In which case, it's best to push on through and pursue your sporting goals relentlessly, irrespective of public opinion, real or feared; of what your so-called mates think about your ambition; or, in today's begrudging world, of what the trolls may say about you on Twitter.

I urge you to grab your opportunity to be great by its lapels. Be that dandy highwayman, for he's right you know - ridicule really is nothing to be scared of.

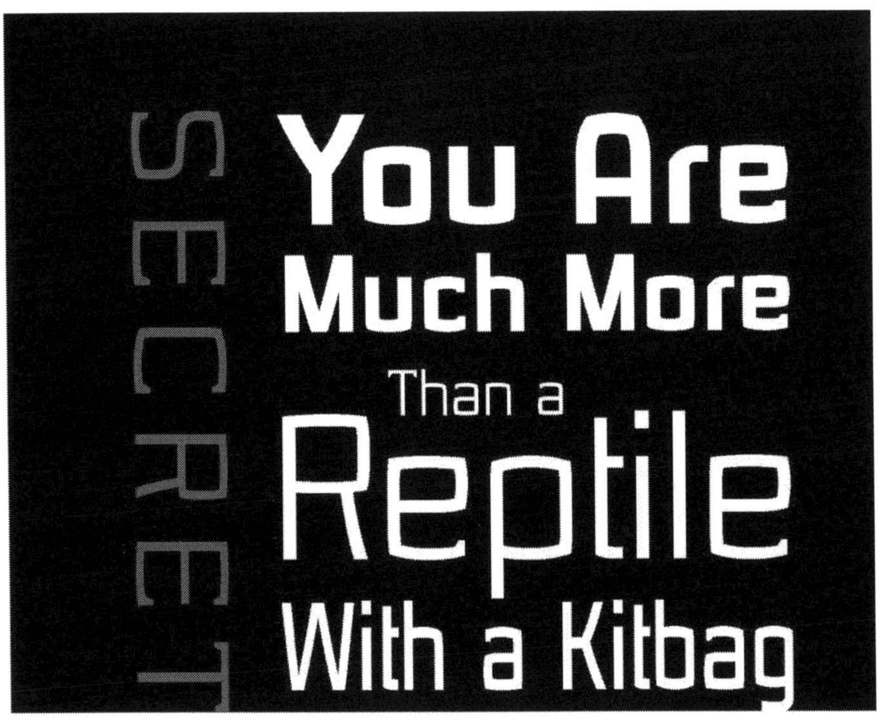
SECRET
You Are
Much More
Than a
Reptile
With a Kitbag

16

As strange as it may sound, you actually have three brains, each one an evolutionary advance on the previous one. They are:

1) The Reptilian Brain (also known as the 'R-Complex') - your surveillance and survival brain.
2) The Limbic System - your emotional brain.
3) The Neocortex - your thinking, logical brain.

Now, for the purposes of this section, I want to focus solely on the reptilian brain and how it has the capacity to devastate your inner game, thereby destroying your outer one.

The Reptilian brain may be ancient, but it remains incredibly powerful. It is our primordial sniffer dog and the seat of our basic drives.

As its fundamental role is to keep us alive, it smells threats to our security and safety, while also regulating such basic life-support functions as breathing, circulation, digestion, sleep, the stress response, and reproduction.

The reptilian brain's focus on self-preservation drives human behaviours related to:

- Territoriality, competing and hostility.
- Status, reputation and social superiority.

You can understand from this how the Frankenstein Factor feeds and threatens these fundamental, primitive needs and drives. There is a definite link between the creation of our mental monster and the function of the reptilian brain.

In evolutionary terms, the reptilian brain (let's call it 'Rep') affords us a significant advantage. After all, it scans our environment for risk and can act with remarkable speed to keep us out of harm's way. For example, if you've ever jumped back off the road to the safety of the pavement, propelled by something instinctive - and just before the unseen car would've hit you - then you can be assured that it was Rep that saved you. And it did so by hijacking your brain.

No way could Rep allow your higher level neocortex to manage the situation. There was simply no time for thinking, just acting. Clearly, in such instances, we are kept safe by the reptilian brain doing its job to the full. So far so good, then.

However, and this is a big HOWEVER, Rep has had its primitive wires crossed. Its role has diversified over the millennia to not only protect us from physical threats - the mastodons and sabre-toothed cats of long ago, through to the speeding vehicles of modern times - but also to keep us safe from threats to our incredibly delicate egos.

Thanks to the Frankenstein Factor, Rep now hijacks the human brain and exerts its control when all that's at risk is a knock to our fragile sense of self-worth. It seems, then, that making mistakes, failing, letting people down, not being liked, or facing ridicule and embarrassment, are the Smilodons of contemporary times.

Now, if we're being really honest, we've all had our moments; times when the reptile rose up within us and all reason was bypassed - when we acted in ways that were completely out of character and disproportionate to the prevailing circumstances, when all that threatened us was some ego-based triviality, such as losing face or having to back down in an argument.

What are we like? I mean, how much have we really evolved?

Given that competitive sport incorporates scrutiny, standards and judgements, the potential for ego-bashing is massive. Unless you are comfortable in your own skin, have a strong mental game, and do not concern yourself with what others may be thinking, then something as relatively benign as making a mistake, or receiving an unfavourable refereeing decision, could be interpreted as 'life threatening' by your confused reptilian brain.

When this happens, things rarely end well. In an effort to get you off the pitch, and back to the sanctuary of the changing room, Rep will rear its scaly head and trigger your fight-or-flight response. This is one mixed-up reptile!

Clearly under such circumstances Rep's hijacking of your neocortex is not useful at all. The threat is merely to the ego, not to survival. Given what is truly important - health, family, love, relationships and fulfilment - it's an absolute shame that many of us waste time worrying about what others think of us.

But the world's best athletes go about things differently. They decontaminate their belief system to rid themselves of ego-related attitudes and thoughts, and build up a mindset that espouses humility, self-motivation and a love of their sport.

With the ego exiled, these elite athletes have, in effect, restricted Rep's influence to its original purpose, as a built-in life-support machine.

So remember, you are much more than a lizard in Lycra or a reptile with a kit bag!

Millions of years have been spent shaping and sculpting your neocortex, your fantastic thinking brain. Learn to use it constructively.

In its efforts to prevent you from achieving your potential, as improving yourself brings with it the risk of failure and derision, your inner monster will spin you the lie that ability is fixed at birth. That your capacity to excel in sport and life is predetermined. If this is happening to you, then you'll probably see talent as some sort of genetic rabbit's foot that propels certain lucky people on to success. You'll even believe that talent is preset and static and therefore not open to change.

17 But those who think in this way live a life of limitation; while those who think big thoughts about their ability to achieve great things, are infinitely more likely to attain success and

fulfilment. The seed of success is therefore in believing that you can. Henry Ford was right, then, when he said: "*If you think you can do a thing or think you can't do a thing, you're right.*"

If you think that effort is worth it, that you can improve your ability to perform in sport, then you will do the work required. By adopting this mindset you will set in motion the requisite motivation and commitment to realise your goals.

However, if deep down you believe that talent is preordained and that putting in hard work, and receiving great coaching really isn't worth it, then guess what, you'll not involve yourself in any meaningful way with any programme of self-development.

The good news is that the talent runes are *not* cast in the womb - rather, *you* are in charge of how skilled you become in any field. *You* are much more in charge of your destiny than many myths would have you believe. And let me tell you, it all starts with Big Thinking. Thinking that links endeavour to reward; that espouses the connection between great coaching, quality practice and greatness itself.

As the business magnate Donald Trump tells us: "*I like thinking big. If you're going to be thinking anything, you might as well think big.*"

And he's right!

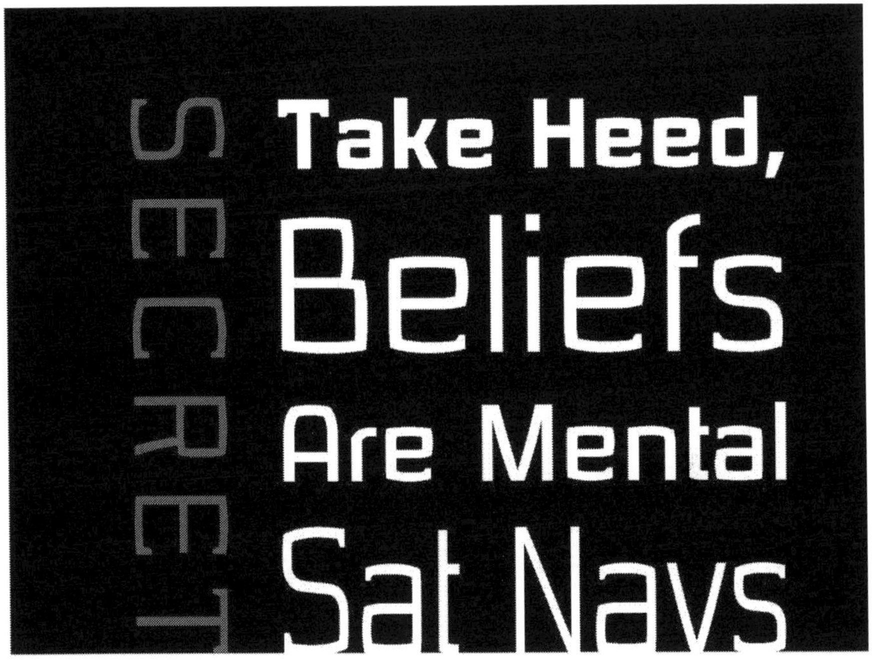
SECRET
Take Heed,
Beliefs
Are Mental
Sat Navs

18

Beliefs are the opinions we hold as true about ourselves, other people, and the world around us. As our mental Sat Navs they give direction to our actions. They steer our minds towards finding supporting evidence for what we believe, while filtering out conflicting information.

This is great, of course, if the beliefs we hold are constructive and help us travel in the direction of our goals. But often, due to the influence of the Frankenstein Factor, many of the beliefs we hold about things tend to be unhelpful and set us on a course in the opposite direction to our dreams.

Here's a quick example of how our core beliefs

(those deep-seated, well-rehearsed opinions that we hold) can have an immediate impact on our self-talk, and in turn on our feelings and behaviour. I was sixteen at the time and attending my first disco. I was a self-conscious kid and believed that I wasn't attractive to girls; that they wouldn't go for the likes of little old me. So, when a beautiful young girl, in colourful 80's garb, smiled over at me, this belief kicked-in and twisted my thinking. In a matter of a second or two, I'd told myself that it couldn't be me she was motioning towards (my interpretation), and as a result I felt a bit deflated (my emotional reaction). I then looked behind me to see who the hunk was that she was really looking at (my behavioural response), but, guess what? There was a wall behind me. No-one was there. It was me after all! She was looking at *me*. In an instant, I turned around with the intention of approaching her. But she was gone.

While not the end of the world, it was clear that I had created my own missed opportunity. Though I had a goal of meeting someone nice that evening, my mental sat nav had a belief keyed-in to it that, unless addressed, was always going to lead me in the opposite direction.

The lesson I eventually learned from this episode is one that has been adopted by the world's most successful people - *If we are to be successful, we must align our beliefs with our goals*. It's sad, but for many people, including athletes, there is a mismatch between the things they would love to accomplish and their underlying opinions about their chances of doing so.

This secret is really important.

For instance, if you have set a goal to make the national squad this season, but simultaneously hold beliefs that you're not the kind of person capable of such an achievement, or that you'll never be good enough to realise this aspiration, then you'll not make the grade.

You must key-in more helpful beliefs/directions into your mental sat nav, or you'll fail.

Quality athletes make use of this secret to offer themselves a considerable advantage over their rivals. They know that there must be a strong alignment between where they want to go in their careers and the beliefs that they hold. Therefore, they work really hard on understanding themselves, teasing out their core beliefs and altering or binning those that are unsupportive. In Secret 20 you will discover how they do this.

SECRET Exploit Frankl's Space

I'm not sure how you viewed life as you were growing up, but I admit that I tended not to see the join between events and my reactions to them. From my perspective it appeared that my emotions and behaviour were run by whatever was going on around me.

Events would occur and, hey presto, I'd feel anxious, sad, frustrated, happy, excited, irritated or whatever. It seemed that situations caused my feelings, that I was a puppet and the outside world pulled my emotional strings. Many people I work with report this same phenomenon; that they believe themselves to be toothless victims of what life throws their way. Stuff happens and they react like automatons, powerless to stop the tide of emotional and behavioural change. They also notice no space between event and emotional response. To be honest, though, there really doesn't appear to be one.

But this is yet another illusion.

There is a space - 'Frankl's space' - and it's infinitely powerful.

Frankl's space is the gap between:

- An **event** that occurs in your environment (e.g. as a golfer, you miss a two-foot putt for par); and,
- Your **reaction** to it (e.g. self-condemnation, anger, dejection, wayward tee shot on the next hole).

I named this space after the eminent Austrian neurologist and psychiatrist, Viktor E. Frankl. He was a Holocaust survivor who, in the midst of witnessing and experiencing unspeakable horrors, searched for some sort of understanding that would offer at least a modicum of meaning to the nightmare. As he considered the hell on earth of the concentration camps, he discovered an invisible space where the guards could not enter, but that was within the reach of every incarcerated man, woman and child.

Writing in his 1946 book, *Man's Search for Meaning*, Frankl explained that:

> *"Even though conditions such as lack of sleep, insufficient food and various mental stresses may suggest that the inmates were bound to react in certain ways, in the final analysis it becomes clear that the sort of person the prisoner became was the result of an inner decision and not the result of camp influences alone."*

What Frankl is saying here is that even in the midst of palpable horror, we still retain the right to think in ways that either weaken us or strengthen us. That we all have the chance to interpret our circumstances in ways which keep us sane, even if the world around us is clearly insane. And the place where we carry out our interpretations is Frankl's space. Frankl explained it in this way:

> *"Between stimulus and response there is a space. In that space is our power to choose our response. In our response lie our growth and our freedom."*

The secret, therefore, is to understand that reality is an inside job. Now, I don't mean that nothing exists in the outside world. Rather, what I am saying is that your experience of what is happening around you is entirely a product of how you interpret events - and not the events themselves.

As an ambitious athlete you really need to make use of Frankl's space. After all, the world's best sports performers take advantage of its mind-changing power. They use the space to gain control over their emotions, beliefs, focus, motivation, performance and career.

The simple, but empowering truth is that ALL situations are emotion-neutral until you think about them.

The golfer, in the example above, who misses that two-foot putt for par needs to wake up to the fact that he has a choice. That he can either take his traditional route by telling himself it should never have happened, that he's a useless golfer and that his tournament is now as good as over. Or instead he can decide to cut himself some slack, by reminding himself that the putt's now in the past, albeit a few seconds ago, and while it is disappointing to bogey the hole, it's not disastrous.

Of course, the golfer needs to know that he has this choice; that he's in charge of his interpretation of the shot. That he has access to Frankl's space and can influence the degree to which he will be affected by the error.

It's the case that athletes who deliver consistently high levels of performance, have learned to interpret their sporting world in profoundly different ways to their underperforming competitors. They fill Frankl's space with constructive, compassionate and self-affirming interpretations, and in doing so, boost their confidence, composure and concentration.

This secret's big message is that *you can control your life*. It doesn't have to control you. As a human being, you have been born with the gift of interpretation and choice.

So, don't squander it. Don't waste the space!

SECRET
Review
and
Refine
Your Mental
Rule Book

You know the saying that we all have a book inside of us - well it's true. Literally! You see, we all have a 'Mental Rule Book' stored in our mind, one which contains all of our beliefs or *rules* for navigating through life.

Though you may not have been aware of the 'writing' process, you've been documenting all sorts of opinions and beliefs into your rule book, from a very young age.

20

Now, hopefully, many of these beliefs serve you well and bolster your efforts to reach your goals in life. But in view of the pernicious nature of the Frankenstein Factor (see Secrets 1, 2 and 3), it is highly likely that you have some beliefs in your Rule Book that work against you and sabotage your attempts to better yourself.

Given the influence of your beliefs on *all* that you do, it is vital that you quality assure the entries in your Mental Rule Book. This way you can identify, challenge and change those beliefs that diminish your chances of attaining your objectives, and retain and refine those that are supportive.

But how do you go about doing this? Well, a good starting point is to monitor and record the negative things you say to yourself, and to document when and where they occur. Next, you should examine and scan these negative statements for core commonalities and themes.

For example, beneath such negative self-talk as:

- *"That was a woeful shot - you're terrible."*
- *"Oh no, another loss. My coach and parents will be ashamed of me."*
- *"I'll never beat him; he's just too good for players like me."*
- *"I hate it when he gets all the attention."*

...may lie beliefs as varied as:

- *"Making mistakes means I'm a bad person."*
- *"It is a dreadful thing to let people down/not meet their expectations."*
- *"I'm just not one of life's winners."*
- *"I should always be top dog."*

As your beliefs steer your thoughts, and your thoughts shape your feelings and actions, then you can see how these kinds of beliefs can lead to a toxic cocktail of anxiety, frustration, self-loathing, guilt, fear, limitation, unhappiness, avoidance and failure. Not the basis, I think you'd agree, from which to launch a dream of being a sporting great!

Once you have identified a negative belief, you should then set about questioning its accuracy with vigour. Use logic and common sense to challenge it, before then changing it into an altogether more useful and truthful rule. For example, the unhelpful, *"It is unacceptable to make mistakes."* could be changed to the more accommodating, *"As I am human, I will make mistakes. To expect otherwise is no way to live."* Clearly, this refinement is much less restrictive and rigid and provides scope for making, accepting and moving on from errors.

By applying the 'challenge and change' method to all of your identified negative beliefs, you will, in effect, be crafting an up-to-date edition of your Mental Rule Book - one full of healthy beliefs that line up neatly behind your goals. This process is central to the mental game work carried out by the world's best athletes, who know only too well that mental toughness is built on a robust belief system.

SECRET
Develop an inner
Judge Judy

21

If you haven't seen Judge Judy Sheindlin in full flow in her reality television court show, then you really are missing a trick. A no-nonsense, articulate and highly logical lawyer, she is able to rip a complaint apart by challenging it in a systematic and persistent way. She's also dispassionate and assertive in her pursuit of truth and justice. Nothing will get in the way of the evidence; and that's how it should be, of course. Not only in the courtrooms of the world, but also in our inner world, where all sorts of slander, defamation, and harassment can take place, typically unopposed.

There's no doubt, we are skilled self-bullies and -harassers. We seldom leave ourselves alone, preferring instead to call ourselves names, and to worry about all sorts of things - few (if any) of which ever happen. What's more, we tend to leave the majority of these complaints and concerns unchallenged, while at the same time hoping to achieve great things! We've no chance.

Are you a bit like this? Well if you are, you need to start to confront your negative thoughts and inner critic head-on. And there's no better way to do this, than to adopt Judge Judy's adversarial approach. So, rather than casually accepting the negative stuff that runs amok in your mind, you will begin to challenge and question it. You will scrutinise it to see if it holds any water.

International surfing star, Ronan Oertzen, is an athlete who has benefited greatly from developing an inner Judge Judy. He puts his negative thoughts in the dock and interrogates them thoroughly to see if they're based on any evidence, or are simply instances of self-heckling:

> *"Self-talk is so powerful. Sometimes when I am having a bad surf and I am not performing well, negative thoughts come into my mind (e.g. 'You will never turn pro', 'Everyone else is better than you'). These types of thoughts really destroy your confidence. To gain my confidence again I question my bad thoughts for proof that they are facts. Every single time there is never any proof."* - Personal communication.

Another one of my clients is the World Number One handball player, Paul Brady. Paul, like Ronan, works hard at managing his thoughts. He has become skilled at weeding out thoughts that are not up to standard and which need to be modified, or binned altogether, as no evidence exists to back them up:

> *"It's just a case of constant monitoring of my thoughts and quelling any doubts as they arise. The main thing is to be aware*

of these negative thoughts and feelings in the lead up to big matches. I usually acknowledge them, analyse them as truthfully and objectively as I can and then begin the process of finding something positive." - Personal communication.

It's really important to remember that the overwhelming majority of your unhelpful thoughts will be irrational and can be easily disputed and changed. But you can only discover this for yourself if you actively monitor your self-talk, and challenge those thoughts that undermine and stress you.

SECRET Know That Success Isn't Always About Winning

How do you define success? Is it solely down to whether or not you win? Is your sense of self-worth directly related to the outcome of your performances? Have you been indoctrinated into the Cult of Results (see Secret 51)?

There's no doubt about it, we're a results obsessed society and hold a very narrow definition of what success looks like. No shades of grey; just winning versus losing; passing versus failing; perfect versus imperfect. This 'either/or' way of thinking about success is adopted by many of us. But we need to be careful, as this rigid mindset is exceptionally unhealthy. For the athlete, it can have a profoundly negative impact upon his self-esteem and lead to low mood, lethargy and depression. By having only one measure of success - *winning* - the athlete's sense of personal value or worth will be eroded each time he loses. Without sufficient room to measure his efforts in a much more balanced way, he is likely to engage in some wounding self-talk and negative reflection. His motivation will suffer and his frustration will be all too evident to those around him.

Sadly, even when he *does* win, he's only borrowing the feel-good factor until his next defeat, when it'll be replaced by dejection. In effect, an athlete with this mentality becomes a type of emotional marionette with two strings; one for success and one for failure. His emotional health will therefore depend on which one is pulled. An outcome over which he may have little or no control.

But, true to form, top rated athletes approach the concept of success in a much more sophisticated manner. Realising that winning is not fully within their control, they turn their attention to the activity that is - their *performance*. Through setting pragmatic, precise and measurable performance goals, they place themselves in charge of their success. After all, the standards set are personal to them and, as such, are within their gift to achieve.

It also means they can still derive significant satisfaction and a sense of achievement from a defeat. It's true! For instance, an 800 metre runner who crosses the line in fourth place (just outside of the medals) can still feel delighted at securing a personal best time.

You see, athletes on the rise have learned to redefine success as something beyond, something deeper, than winning a race, match or tournament. That's not saying they don't want to win. Of course they do. But a broader definition of what success can look like, vastly increases the probability of winning. That's the beautiful irony; take your focus off winning and winning is more likely!

When you start setting performance goals, you will find that a positive shift occurs in your levels of motivation and commitment. These goals are yours and, as such, are both within your control and realisable. Any fear around failing will evaporate, as your point of attention has moved away from fretting over outcomes and instead rests on performance *processes*.

You'll also feel a renewed enthusiasm for training. As you now hold the levers to goal-attainment, you will want to learn from your displays and work on those areas that need refined. With this 'learning and doing' mentality, it will only be a matter of time before competitive wins start to accrue and a progression through the ranks is set in motion.

And all from being smart in how you define success.

SECRET
Know the
Difference Between
Healthy
and Unhealthy
Competitiveness

23

To excel at sport, you need to be competitive. That's obvious. However, what many athletes don't know is that it needs to be a certain type of competitiveness - a *healthy* competitiveness, as cultivated by the world's finest athletes.

So, what is it? Well, 'healthy competitiveness' is a mature mindset. It sees competition as a personal challenge and an opportunity to gauge progress, learn and improve. There's no preoccupation with what others are thinking and doing, no obsessing about rivals' performances, and no pleasure taken whenever they fail. Jealousy, hostility and bitterness are alien emotions. Instead, the 'healthy competitor' respects his opponents and wishes them well. He is humble in victory and generous in defeat, and won't expend valuable energy seething over a loss to his nearest challenger. Instead, he will review his display, learn from it and redouble his efforts in training. It's all focused on him, and his improvement; not on others, and their successes or failures.

However, 'unhealthy competitiveness' comes from an altogether darker place. It's an attitude with a host of toxic traits - jealousy being the most venomous of the lot. An athlete with this twisted mindset spends far too much time dwelling on the progress of his fellow competitors and, in doing so, fails to attend to what *he* needs to do to improve *his own* game. This split screen focus is next to useless, if your goal is to be the best in your sport.

Remember, champions place their full attention on *their* progress and the work *they* need to get on with. They refuse to dabble in the juvenile, nasty and profoundly destructive ways of the unhealthy competitor.

Okay, time for a bit of honesty. Hand on heart, which side of the healthy/unhealthy divide are you on? Does your competitiveness come from a pure and mature place, or is its source tainted and childish? If it's mostly the former, then this is very good news, and you are starting you journey to world-class mental toughness and ability from a solid base. But, if it is mostly the latter, then you really must do something about it, otherwise your unhealthy competitiveness will ruin your career, lose you friends and, if you're not careful, lead to illness. Your inner revolution, from 'unhealthy' to 'healthy' competitor', involves a process of extricating your focus away from the accomplishments of other people, away from resentment, and back to the very beginning. Back to your true self. The self you were born with, who took up sport for the right reason - for pleasure, personal challenge and growth.

SECRET
Surround
Yourself
With Good
People

24

There is a witticism that goes something like this: "Behind every successful man is a surprised woman". Well, behind every successful athlete is a support network. The surprise is that the majority of sports performers try to go it alone. But it's not sustainable. No matter what tales you have been spun by the media, the best in any field - be it sport, medicine, business or entertainment - didn't reach the top on their own.

The best never travel alone, and I don't mean in planes, trains or automobiles! Instead they have a cohort of expert advisers, coaches, mentors, family and friends, all of whom have bought into the vision, and who offer unconditional encouragement, constructive criticism and guidance as the journey towards greatness unfolds.

What about you? As you work towards your goals, do you have enough support? Or do you feel on your own? Is your coach fully committed to helping you? Are your family and friends aware of your ambition? Have you disclosed your goals to them? If not, why not? Do you believe they'll not offer you the backing you need? In fact, do you believe that it's a sign of weakness to have such support in the first place? If this is your belief, then challenge it.

If you haven't got support, then I urge you to do something to address the situation. Write out the names of the people who are important to you and who could play a pivotal role in providing the support you need. Then go and speak to them. Do not underestimate the authority of a heartfelt request for help.

To have people on your side will add power to your life and sporting dreams.

SECRET
Outride
the Four
Horsemen
of the
Apocalypse

From his extensive research into relationships, world-renowned marriage expert, Dr. John Gottman, has identified four negative attitudes and behaviour patterns that predict divorce. He has named these the 'Four Horsemen of the Apocalypse', a reference to the four portents of doom in the Bible. Gottman claims that the predictors of breakup and divorce are: *criticism*, *contempt*, *defensiveness*, and *stonewalling*.

25

If these noxious behaviours are elicited by either partner, then, without being remedied, it's highly probable the relationship will fail. Bear with me for a moment, as I briefly set out each of the four attitudes and behaviours. (The relevance of these to you and sport will follow):

CRITICISM: Here you attack your partner's character to assert that the problem lies with him or her.

CONTEMPT: This is the most ferocious of the horsemen. Contempt is a deliberate display of cruelty directed at your partner's core self. It will involve name-calling, mocking, and being sarcastic. It's an all-out assault on the other person's sense of being and can be the overspill from months or years of pent-up views and frustrations.

DEFENSIVENESS: This is the failure to take responsibility for your own role in the problem. It's an attitude that points the finger at the other person. Always the other person's fault; never you!

STONEWALLING: Here you avoid maturing, in what can be an unfair and uncertain world. It's an attitude that ensures you disengage from the elephant in the room - the troubled relationship. You will use all sorts of ruses to withdraw from the relationship. Perhaps you'll go out more often without your partner, sit in silence when in the house and, if issues are raised, immediately change the subject to something much less threatening.

While Gottman's Four Horsemen are harbingers of marital instability, this gruesome foursome can just as easily rampage through another one of life's pivotal relationships - *the one we have with ourselves* - and leave many of us in a state of personal instability.

For an athlete intent on achieving great things in sport, inner stability is an absolute 'must have'. A sports performer who is at war with himself is extremely unlikely to cope with the 'no place to hide' nature of the competitive setting, where his insecurity could be exposed for all to see, particularly during those more critical moments when the match isn't going his way. At these times of perceived crises (for example, after committing an error) his self-loathing and self-blame will increase. And this is also how things unfold within a fractured marital relationship. When it's exposed to too many crises, such as financial or health difficulties, it will implode. Without stability at its core, it cannot withstand the stresses and strains of life.

In fact, as I write this, it's 'Divorce Day', the third of January. This day turns out to be the most common one for couples to consult their lawyers to instigate divorce proceedings, as the stresses and strains of the festive season have widened the cracks.

Listen out for the sound of hooves

You will know that you're training and performing under the hooves of the Four Horsemen, when you talk to yourself (and others) like this:

> CRITICISM: *"You always mess up and never play well in the really important events."*
>
> CONTEMPT: *"Call yourself a footballer? You're useless. Pathetic."*
>
> DEFENSIVENESS: *"It's not my fault. It was the referee and his stupid decisions: he put me off my game. He's the reason I played badly today."*
>
> STONEWALLING: *"There's nothing wrong with the way I train boss... Hey, did you see where I put my phone?"*

It's a sobering fact, but if you're displaying any or all of these highly destructive attitudes and behaviours, then you are gravely undermining your chances of reaching your goals in sport, let alone living a life of love and fulfilment. Staying ahead of this particularly perilous posse is therefore really important.

So, how do you do it?

Well, first, you must start to treat yourself with respect and kindness. And, second, you really need to take responsibility for your own development and to adopt a mature and accountable approach to tough times. Stop the self-loathing, -blaming and -criticising.

When life and sport don't go your way, stop ripping yourself apart, or allowing your emotions to hijack your common sense. Instead, take a step back, relax your angry, self-critical mind and, in a structured, dispassionate way devise a plan to deal with the problem. Be open and honest with yourself. Don't live in denial. Have the courage to look life in the eye and trust yourself to live it to the full.

Treat yourself as you would do a loved-one. This is the pupa from which all great things emerge - including a fantastic sports career!

SECRET
The Past and Future
Exert a
Gravitational
Pull on Us
Use this Access Wisely

26

Having had our left hemisphere stretched by the education system, it's not surprising that the vast majority of us possess a preponderance of left brain traits. One such characteristic is the way in which it processes time. While our right brain is much more concerned with the present, our left hemisphere's preoccupation is with the *past* and *future*. It trawls through past experiences to help inform the present, and to forecast what's going to happen next. Which, you must remember, could be the outcome of the penalty kick you're about to take in five second's time! Used wisely, this left brain function can be a fantastic asset for the athlete.

For instance, take a golfer (let's call him *Golfer 1*) who is lining up a 10-foot putt to win a big tournament. He is mentally tough, and knows to dip into his memory bank and select an example or two of having successfully clinched such clutch putts in the past. He cleverly uses his memory to inform the present and to boost his confidence for the shot he's about to take. There is no other self-talk. No need. His left brain has done its bit and butts out, allowing the quiet and in-the-moment focus of his right brain to take over. Nothing else exists for this player, just the task-at-hand. With his focus trained on the stroke, the putt is smoothly hit and the ball rolls in the hole. Being smart in how he uses his brain leads *Golfer 1* to victory.

Now, let's change the golfer to a guy with an untrained brain, someone who has, so far, shunned mental game training. What's likely to happen as this player lines up the putt? Well, it could go something like this.

Faced with the very same putt to win, this particular player - *Golfer 2* - becomes overwhelmed by an avalanche of miserable memories that remind him of previous failures and his tendency to choke. He recalls the short putt he missed to make the cut a week ago and how, the previous year, he'd let a three-stroke lead slip at the eighteenth hole.

Memory after memory floods his mind and his anxiety goes through the roof. His hands tremble and he's desperate to just get it all over with. He strikes the ball clumsily and it's no surprise when it sails past its target. Unable to eradicate this miss from his mind, he proceeds to also miss the return putt. With his game unravelling and victory thrown away, he putts out for a bogey, before then sloping off the course disconsolate and with head bowed.

The difference between Golfers 1 and 2 is not to be found in their technical ability, but rather their inner game. Where *Golfer 1* spends time building up a mental catalogue of positive memories, times when he performed with excellence, *Golfer 2* simply didn't know to do this, and therefore left his emotional state and focus to chance. He allowed his past experiences to pollute his present and ruin his performance. The secret then, is to make your memory work for you. You need to organise your own back catalogue of successes, before then committing each one to memory. There are two steps to this task:

Step 1. Look back over your performances and note down specific instances of excellence; times when you performed just as you had wanted to. If you have been carrying out performance reviews, and keeping them in a journal, then you'll already have the information at-hand, and can select examples from it.

Step 2. Commit your examples to memory by tagging them with a highly positive emotion. The human brain is more inclined to store those events and experiences that are accompanied by strong emotional states. The emotion 'tells' the brain that the incident is too important to forget. So, replay your examples of performance excellence in your mind's eye, and, as you watch them, feel great about what you're witnessing. Tag each one with a type of mental fist pump. Don't hold back. This is not a time for modesty.

By adding on an upbeat response (one that cries out, "Wow, that was a terrific serve/save/throw/tackle/pass/goal!") to each example, you'll be embedding the memory more fully, thereby making it more accessible at crucial times during competition, as illustrated by Golfer 1 above.

What's more, your brain will want to repeat these moments of excellence, as doing so clearly pleases its boss - YOU!

SECRET 27
Know That Concentration is Never Lost Just Misplaced

Athletes, like many of us, will complain that a particular performance didn't go well because, at crucial moments, they had *lost* their focus. But they hadn't. It can't be lost!

To illustrate this secret more fully, listen-in to the following conversation which took place after one of my clients, a leading amateur golfer, asked for a quick word before he headed off for a bite to eat. Let's call him Phil.

Phil: "I'm so unhappy with my scoring today. It's my focus. It was completely gone out on the course today Mark. That hasn't happened for a very long time."

ME: "Okay Phil, sorry to hear that. But all's not

lost, including your focus. I mean, where do you think it went?

Phil: "What do you mean? Sure I told you, I lost it."

ME: "Well, if your concentration hadn't been lost, as you put it, where would it have been?"

Phil: "Well, it should've been on my shots. The one I've to hit next, and not on the mistakes I've made, or who's doing what on the leader board... "

ME: "Exactly. Rather than being lost, your focus was actually working really well, but on the wrong stuff. You had misplaced it, putting it on to other things - errors, results, and other people - and so you distracted yourself from the shot-at-hand."

Phil: "Ah, right. My concentration was switched on, but not on my game. I get it. Focus is never really lost, just badly used."

ME: "Yes. Always remember this - and it's a secret the top guys in sport know - distraction is not the absence of concentration, but an inappropriate placing of it, usually to internal matters; things such as worries, regrets and self-criticism. You have to train your mind to pay attention to what really matters at any one moment during a round.

Phil wanted to work on this part of his mental game as soon as possible, as all eager athletes do. Therefore, not long after our conversation, Phil and I sat down together to work on a few simple routines by following the principles set out in Secrets 38 and 39.

SECRET
Train Your
Inner
Cabbie

When all is said and done, what separates the world's best athletes from their rivals is their ability to control their emotional state when it really matters. Mentally tough performers know themselves inside and out.

Top athletes are therefore like London Cabbies - they have the Knowledge.

28

They know their emotional landscape with the same sort of fantastic detail as London's premier taxi drivers know their city. They have such an intimate understanding of their emotional topography that they never get lost for too long, if at all. Though they take the occasional wrong turn, they recognise it immediately and do a quick reverse. They don't sit revving their engine in a mental and emotional dead-end; instead, they turn things around, regain their composure and switch to cruise control.

To develop your own inner cabbie, you must study your emotional landscape in painstaking detail, with the aim of identifying two key pieces of information:

1. The **destination** (i.e. your Personal Ideal Performance State - PIPS).
2. The **best route** (i.e. the techniques you can use to reach your PIPS).

Knowledge really is power.

To identify your PIPS, you must pore over some of your performances. Two kinds in particular should be examined: peak performances and poor performances. By comparing and contrasting your best and worst competitive displays, you can begin to piece together your 'just right' emotional state for competition.

As you carry out this exercise, you should begin to notice a distinct pattern emerging from the information. For instance, you may discover that prior to your *weak performances* you had a tendency to be highly anxious, irritable, or overly concerned about making mistakes. Or that you were frequently sick in the toilets and experienced palpitations or other uncomfortable symptoms of stress. Maybe a poor display was actually preceded by a really flat mood and lethargy.

When you turn your attention to your *high level performances*, you should note that things were a whole lot more positive and focused in the lead up to competition. You may remember feeling much more energised, excited and confident at these times; that you had a 'bring it on' attitude, and weren't side-tracked by irrelevancies.

This task is incredibly empowering, as it not only helps you to identify your PIPS, but it also demonstrates how this ideal state has a hugely positive impact upon your performance in competition. And equally, how an unprepared mind and inadequate mental state can destroy your performance.

By pinpointing your PIPS you are providing your inner cabbie with a specific destination - the emotional place you need to arrive at, before competition begins. With this ideal state identified, you can then set about learning arousal management techniques and designing routines and preparation plans that will ensure you reach your PIPS consistently, and on time! (See Secrets 29, 30 and 35).

SECRET
Know the
Quickest
Route to
Your PIPS

29

Elite athletes will not fall victim to their emotions. They will not passively accept the mood they're in, if it isn't going to produce a top performance. Instead, they use a range of techniques to adjust their arousal to the right level; either boosting it, if it's too flat or lowering it, if it's too high.

Here we see the significance of Secret 28.

Having spent time identifying their PIPS, the world's best athletes know when it's missing, and can respond instantly to remedy the situation. To do this, they make use of well-rehearsed techniques to adjust their level of arousal to the ideal state.

These strategies are invaluable and I urge you to learn them. Here are some great examples:

1. Techniques to use when you are highly anxious, uptight and worried:
   - **Abdominal breathing** (see Secret 30).
   - **Calming Imagery** (see Secret 54).
   - **The Ticker-tape Technique** (see Secret 48).
   - **Constructive thinking** (see Secrets 19, 20, 21 and 45).

You should also consider learning the art of Meditation, as well as Progressive Muscle Relaxation. Check to see if there are any classes run in your neighbourhood.

2. Techniques to use when you feel sluggish and need a boost to your motivation:
   - **Mood Music:** Music is a mood-enhancing 'drug', so use it. Have a Top 10 of songs or tunes, any one of which will increase your arousal level.
   - **Physical activity:** Complete short energetic bursts of activity, such as stretching and running on the spot.
   - **Breathing method:** Engage in short, shallow breathing to stimulate your physiology and psychological state.
   - **Motivational Imagery:** Use imagery to place your mind in exciting situations, and to increase your arousal level for competition. For instance, if you are a goalkeeper, visualise yourself coming for a corner kick, springing into the air, and feeling the football firmly in your gloved hands, before then bringing it into your chest. Hear the crowd applaud and really feel your excitement build.
   - **Motivational DVDs:** Watch and listen to an inspirational DVD. Better still, produce one yourself. A bespoke video will

push more of your emotional buttons than an off-the-shelf example.

- **Positive self-talk:** There are times when you really need to give yourself a good old pep talk, one that stiffens the sinews, summons up the blood, and stimulates your competitive juices. Be your own motivational guru and coax yourself towards your PIPS.

World number one handball player Paul Brady is adept at such self-cajoling:

> "*While I try to make sure I'm not flat in the first place, when it does occur I remind myself of how hard I have trained... I sit down and write out the reasons why I deserve to win or why I should be motivated to win.*" - Personal communication.

Top athletes realise that their PIPS is a personal thing, and so select the strategies and techniques that work best for them. Let's return to handball legend, Paul Brady, and read his description of his regime and how he reaches his ideal state:

> "*I usually adopt various different strategies when dealing with pre-match nerves. During the week leading into a big match/tournament, I try to stay as relaxed as possible and to put things in perspective if I am feeling overly anxious. I reframe my thinking and try to remind myself to <u>enjoy the challenge</u> that lies ahead. I convince myself (most often unsuccessfully!) that it is only a game at the end of the day, even though it doesn't feel like that at the time. On the day of a match I again try to stay as relaxed as possible by focusing on a few key points:*
>
> - *Breathing - slow, deep breaths*
> - *Keep on the balls of my feet*

- *Listen to my iPod*

Go over key points in my mind again and again." - Personal communication.

As Paul demonstrates, behind greatness are solid routines that act like scaffolding to hold the mind in place in advance of and during competition. Work hard at this area of your mental game. It's vital.

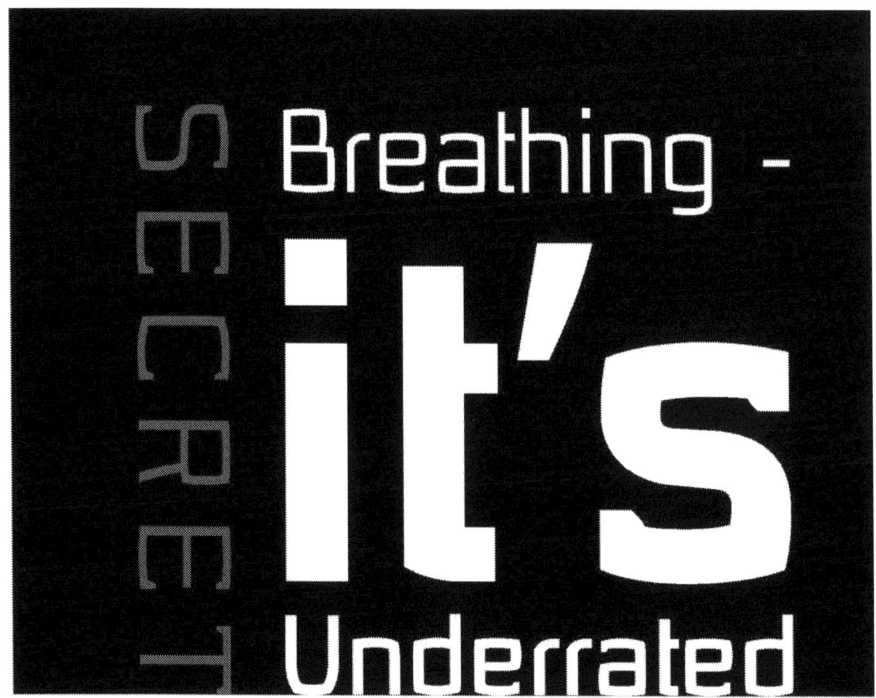
SECRET
Breathing -
it's
Underrated

30

One of the simplest, yet most powerful ways for an athlete to control his emotional state is to breathe properly. Abdominal breathing can soothe an anxious mind and settle a tense and tight body.

However, many athletes breathe in a way that actually intensifies their arousal levels beyond what is comfortable and conducive to peak performance. They breathe from their chests, not their stomachs. By doing this, they generate short, shallow and irregular breaths.

When we breathe from the stomach our breaths are slow, deep and even. This boosts the movement of oxygen around the body, enhances neural messaging, improves muscle functioning and calms a fretful psyche.

This is good for performance.

So, let's assess your breathing style. To do this, place one hand on your stomach and one hand on your chest - then take several good breaths. Breathe in and let it out, and notice which one of your hands moves the most on the inhalation. Is it the 'tummy hand' or the 'chest hand'? Which seems to fill up with air?

If your stomach expands, then great, your breathing style is really going to help you out. You have a highly effective mental game tool at your disposal, one that can improve your readiness to perform, and keep you focused during competition.

Now, if your chest expands on the inhalations, then you have identified something very important - you are not maximising the oxygen flow within your brain and body. It's therefore time to learn the proper method, one I have named the *4-2-4 Technique*. It will help you to quell anxiety on-the-spot.

4-2-4 Technique

Find a comfortable place to sit or stand, and where you will not be disturbed. Next, breathe in slowly and deeply to a count of **4**, ensuring that your abdomen rises and your chest stays still. Hold this breath for **2** seconds, before exhaling to a count of **4**. Purse your lips as you exhale to attain the best result. You'll find that a sense of relaxation will flow throughout your body.

Take what I've just described as a single 4-2-4 repetition, before then completing a further four reps. Assign ten minutes daily to practice this technique for a period of three weeks. You'll find that with regular practice you will not need to use your hands to determine the correctness of your breathing style. You'll be breathing properly and using the 4-2-4 method with great success before and during competition. You will be acting in the very same way as the world's top athletes, who have harnessed their breathing as a fantastically simple tool to manage their emotions.

SECRET Go For The Jab! Mental Inoculation

By introducing a weakened form of a virus into the body, vaccines train the immune system to fight and defeat the actual disease, should it attack at some point in the future. Resilience is built up and the body is primed to cope.

Simulation training is the sport psychology equivalent of a vaccine. It offers an opportunity for an athlete to experience, and successfully deal with, such psychological 'microbes' as:

- Suffering toxic anxiety 10 minutes before kick-off.
- Performing in front of a packed stadium.
- Being mocked by spectators, or slated

by coaching staff and teammates.

- Receiving an unfavourable decision from the match official.
- Stepping up to take a penalty kick, or vital putt.
- The moment after making a mistake.

While there are as many scenarios that can disturb and distract an athlete's mind, as there are athletes in the world, they do all share a common fear - the fear about what other people think. If you want to test this out, jot down your usual distractions and identify the ultimate fear held within each one. I'm sure that you too will find that your underlying concern is largely focused on avoiding ridicule and rejection.

Right, there are two categories of simulated practice - physical and mental. These can help you rehearse for those feared situations, the ones that you really need to manage effectively.

Physical Simulation

Here the athlete takes part in clever mock-ups of those scenarios that tend to side-track him during competition. For example, if he's inclined to feel overwhelmed by performing in front of others, then he or his coach could invite a sizeable group of 'spectators' to training sessions. Family, friends or members of the local media or supporters group could be asked to attend. This simulation should go some way to reproduce the pressure the athlete experiences from being scrutinised and judged. Training under these conditions offers him a considerable taste of what's to come in competition, as well as the opportunity to apply refocusing strategies when he starts to worry about public opinion.

Focusing ability can also be strengthened by introducing various potential distractions into the training setting. For example:

- A golfer could practice against the backdrop of the intermittent clicking of cameras, mobile phones ringing, or a spectator who just cannot stop coughing at inopportune moments.
- The rent-a-crowd collective invited to training could engage in some heckling to unnerve the athlete.
- An ear-splitting crowd recording could be played over the speaker system to condition an inexperienced team as to what lies ahead in a forthcoming big cup game.

Mental Simulation

A great way to complement physical simulation is to use the limitless power of the human imagination. While it can be difficult to reproduce all potential scenarios in the training setting, thanks to the mind's versatility performers can replicate anything mentally. And from the comfort of their own homes!

An imagined situation, vividly created, is received by the human brain as the real thing. The options for simulation are therefore endless. Athletes can see, feel, hear, and otherwise sense themselves succeed in all sorts of performance scenarios. Secret 54 sets out the C.R.E.A.T.E. method for producing effective imagery, while Secret 53 describes the numerous ways in which this technique can be used.

Simulation, physical and mental, is an astonishingly effective form of performance preparation. It's an art, and therefore requires creativity and innovation. So think beyond the well-worn norms of what training should look like. Push the boundaries of preparation and set yourself some mock exams. Nothing beats 'being there' before the real event begins.

SECRET 32: Gain Control by Doing the Mental Toughness Tango

Across the world right now, elite athletes are dancing. Not any old dance, mind you; not even a physical one. Rather, it's a mental toughness tango. This delicate dance is a strategic battle between opposites. It's about the athlete gaining control, while at the same time giving some of it away. It's about learning to influence what he can affect during his preparation and performance, and letting go of the illusion that he can control everything.

How about you - have you learned the mental toughness tango? Are you in charge of your performance? Or do the uncontrollable aspects of your sport tend to trip you up a little too often? Those past errors, for instance, do they pester you, even though they're done and dusted and are therefore unalterable?

Well, if your mental game is more breakdance than tango right now, then I suggest you go back to basics and identify the two protagonists in the dance - the 'controllables' and the 'uncontrollables'.

First off, divide an A4 page into two columns and head them up as 'My Controllables' and 'My Uncontrollables'. Then register, in the relevant column, those factors before and during competition that fall within your control, and those that do not. Carry out this activity and you'll end up with two powerful sets of data; though, here, I want you to focus on your list of 'uncontrollables'. For contained within it, are the immutable situations over which you could waste vital energy and concentration (e.g. adverse weather conditions; suspension in play; poor officiating; unfortunate bounce of the ball; talent scout in the crowd; and, errors).

This list gives you a massive heads up on those aspects of your sporting experience that you really need to accept, and to move on from *immediately*. Approached with the right attitude, you'll find that letting go of these uncontrollable things frees you up from all sorts of unnecessary angst and anxiety. Energy will be saved, as your focus is directed to only those elements of your performance that are under your command. What's more, you'll begin to perform with greater freedom and effectiveness, as your mind has been firewalled off from fixating on the uncontrollable features of the sporting experience.

SECRET
Maximise
Downtime:
Minimise
Stir-craziness

33

A golfer once told me that he felt imprisoned in his own head at certain times during a round. He was jittery before crucial shots and found it incredibly difficult to move on after making a mistake. He came to see me, because it dawned on him that all of the coaching he'd received since he was a kid, had gone towards only 15 per cent of a round of golf - the time when he was actually hitting shots. But nobody had bothered to teach him how to positively approach the remaining 85 per cent, the *downtime* between shots.

To him, this was very strange, because he knew that he and many other golfers suffered badly during these downtime periods. He applied the term 'going a little stir-crazy' to describe how he often felt, particularly when he was playing poorly. He would feel trapped in his own mind by thoughts of failure, the error he'd just made, the heat of public scrutiny, and by feelings of disquiet and despondency.

Over a period of three months, this young golfer made significant progress in his mental game. For the very first time he looked inside for answers. (In the past he'd changed his coach, caddy and clubs in a futile search for an external 'cure'). He spent a couple of weeks monitoring his game and recording those occasions when he went 'stir-crazy'. Once he'd joined up the dots across several rounds of competitive golf, he was able to accept and digest what the best golfers and athletes on the planet have come to know - *Learning to manage downtime (times when there is a break in the competitive action) is a crucial ingredient in the delivery of high level performances.*

When the action stops - even for a few seconds - it is incredibly important to maintain concentration and not allow your mind to wander off. So if you're a footballer, and the match you're playing in is halted while a player receives treatment for an injury, you need to remain focused and prepared to resume your role the second the game is restarted. Standing around worrying about how the game will turn out, what the result will be, or if you'll be substituted later on, will only serve to compromise your mental state and steal your focus away from the present. And it's in the present where the match is taking place.

Never underestimate the damage you can do to your performance during a handful of seconds of downtime. An unchallenged negative thought has the power to bleed into your emotional state and subsequent action - which could well be a penalty kick or a serve at match point.

Athletes who suffer the most during breaks in competition are those with limited mental skills who haven't learned how to manage downtime. These performers tend to fill the interruption in play with all sorts of unhelpful thoughts, surrendering to the solitude, even if the time is short.

To be honest, we all do it, we all have difficulty dealing with solitude - a phenomenon, as you'll know, that has been exploited by prison systems and torturers around the world. Solitary confinement is used as one of the most effective forms of punishment, though the irony is that all the jailer has to do is to provide the cell. The prisoner will do the rest himself!

Now, it's one thing to go stir-crazy during such severe incarceration, which may stretch to months and years, but another thing entirely to do it during sport. I mean, it's only sport for goodness sake. Not exactly the same as being banged up in a Stateside Penitentiary!

Still, I've got to tell you, I've worked with athletes, like the golfer above, who can appear edgy, tense, anxious and, to all intents and purposes, trapped during what can be the briefest of periods during competition. Yes, trapped - by the fear of scrutiny and judgement. Trapped in a prison of their own making. Take the rugby player, for instance, who is on his own in the middle of the pitch, lining up a penalty kick to win the match. Without a strong mental game, he may feel cornered by the force of expectation. With thousands of eyes watching him, a bit of stir-craziness could set in. He may become overly anxious, fidgety and agitated, with his focus on the task-at-hand shifting to a fear of failure.

Then there's the footballer who makes a mistake that results in the opposition scoring. He too may feel alone, isolated by the unsympathetic responses of his teammates and coach, and worried that his error is a harbinger of things to come. As he waits for the restart, he has a crucial decision to make. He can either continue to ruminate on what was, or he can refocus on *what is* - that he's a professional athlete, paid to perform a role and, as the match is about to resume, he'd better get on with things.

An important point to make here is that many athletes are unaware there is a choice available in such circumstances. Or, if they do know, haven't the means to escape their self-imposed mental prison during downtime. But elite performers cover both angles. They realise there's always a choice and have a toolbox of techniques to help them recover their ideal state.

So don't be surprised that the world's top athletes prepare as much for the times when the action stops, as for the actual performance itself.

What about you? Do you have plans in place to manage your downtime? And remember, it encompasses anything from a few seconds during a match, to many minutes at halftime, or an hour on the substitutes' bench. Athletes point to the short time after making an error, as a pivotal second or two of downtime that needs to be managed well. They also refer to the time between points in sports such as tennis, and of course between shots in golf. As a rule of thumb, those sports that have many periods of downtime are generally the most mentally demanding. Not because of the downtime, per se, but because of how we tend deal with it.

While I've heard athletes and psychologists speak of downtime as *causing* problems, it simply doesn't. Athletes cause problems for athletes during these times. Which is why being mentally tough is so incredibly important. It empowers athletes to manage situations in ways that help bolster their performance, not impair it.

34

Here’s a powerful little tip for those moments when you think your world has caved-in: when in fact all that's happened is simply an inconvenience in the heat of competition. Hitting a shanked golf shot or making an ill-timed tackle, for example.

You'll remember from Secret 16, that our lower (reptilian) brain can often hijack our more evolved logical brain and equate these types of sporting slip-ups and inconveniences with an attack on our actual survival, especially when they occur in public view. When this happens, our reactions tend to be extreme and totally disproportionate to the incident. Left unchallenged, we usually go on to commit further errors.

What's needed in these circumstances is a large dose of good old-fashioned perspective. And one way to do this swiftly - before the 'reptile' sends you back to the changing room, or your clubs go in the lake - is to 'Google Earth' the incident. Here, you mentally rise above your problem, by zooming out from it to gain a more rational perspective on what's really happened.

So, while you may have sent your shot wide of the post, landed your ball in the rough, or well and truly messed something up during your performance, it's just a microscopic dot when viewed from above. By zooming out in this way, you can have a really good look around you to see what else is going on.

In your mind's eye, you could 'look across' to the local hospital and zoom right in to see a young patient receiving some very bad news. Or go further down the corridor and hear a doctor say that he has tried everything and can do no more. Maybe you'd zoom in on a starving child searching the landfills, or a mother in a nursing home struggling to recall her son's name.

Although your mind's eye scenario is up to you, I can guarantee you'll gain perspective once you've visualised one of life's true tragedies. Use this technique to release you from the angst of the moment and then just get on with your game. And be really grateful that you can do so.

The Google Earth technique requires a bit of creativity and imagination, but stick with it. It'll literally help you to rise above a performance setback.

SECRET 35 Develop a Preparation Chain

The human brain loves routine. We love routine. It generates a sense of comfort, control and confidence. Yet, it never ceases to amaze me that many athletes fail to capitalise on this trait.

I have found a distinct lack of effort and quality in how athletes prepare for competition. The pre-competition period is often treated with alarming indifference and inconsistency. At best, some trivial rituals are followed. You know the type - the same meal on a Saturday morning, being last to leave the changing room, rolling on the right sock first, and so forth. These are superficial ceremonies and do little to ready the athlete's mind. What's needed instead is a daisy chain of routines that shape mind and body, preparing each in a meticulous way so that the athlete is in his ideal performance state; up for the challenge ahead and ready to give it his all.

Top competitors develop competition plans, a series of activities that connects the before and during phases of performance. By carrying out certain actions in a certain order, they ready themselves in steps. Energy is used wisely, focus remains on relevant issues, and the Personal Ideal Performance State is reached at exactly the right time.

This is a strategic mission that begins with a blank sheet of paper. So grab that pen and paper again and begin to list, in sequence, the steps you will take in the lead-up to match day. Record the routines you'll adhere to on-site, and during performance. Here are some prompts to kindle your thinking:

Period 1 - Night before competition

- Devise a routine that's relaxing and guarantees a good night's sleep. Be specific - note down what you will do, the time you'll go to bed and the hours you want to sleep. You'll discover in Secret 56 the influence sleep has on a sports performance.

Period 2 - Competition day

- Again, be specific in detailing your plans. Here, your activities bridge the period from when you wake up to when you arrive at the stadium, court, track or course. Make sure to set time aside for packing your kitbag and having a final check of its contents. You should also record when and what you'll eat and drink.
- Be certain to schedule in your mental game work. Perhaps you'll spend some minutes visualising crucial skill sets and recalling instances of excellence from your performance memory bank (see Secret 26).

- Record the time you will leave your home or hotel for the competition site, how you will travel, the route you'll take, and the estimated time of arrival.

Period 3 - At the competition site

- To ensure that you cover this important period as constructively as possible, you should draft an On-Site Plan. Note down the physical and mental routines you'll engage in from arrival through to game time. Keep things simple. Have a solid warm-up routine and a tool-box of techniques that'll help you adjust your arousal to your preferred level (see Secrets 29 and 30).
- Write down the strategies you'll employ for dealing with distractions. Make a note of your techniques for focusing and refocusing, as well as the moments when they're likely to be required. Of course, by the time you reach the stadium, you'll have learned these techniques thoroughly. All that'll be necessary at the competition site is for you to run your eye over the methods one final time. Like college examinations, it's one last look at your revision notes before you step into the exam hall.
- Record your contingency plans to manage those 'What if?' moments, should they occur before or during performance. Again, these should be well-rehearsed ahead of time.

This pre-performance preparation chain, as I call it, is a highly significant strategy in its own right. I urge you to discuss your ideas with your coach and to agree a plan that covers as many bases as possible.

A useful way to begin the process is to start with the end in mind. Identify how you want to feel before stepping out to compete, and then work backwards from there. In other words, if you perform at your peak whenever you are nervously excited, then draw up a set of activities and routines that will enable you to reach this desired state. At the end of the day, this is what preparation is meant to achieve - the readiness to perform with the necessary focus, composure and proficiency.

Athletes at the top of their game are meticulous in their preparations and in doing so gain a healthy confidence from knowing that, whatever occurs, they can deal with it. This in itself generates a sense of freedom and flow, a mental state that leads to peak performance.

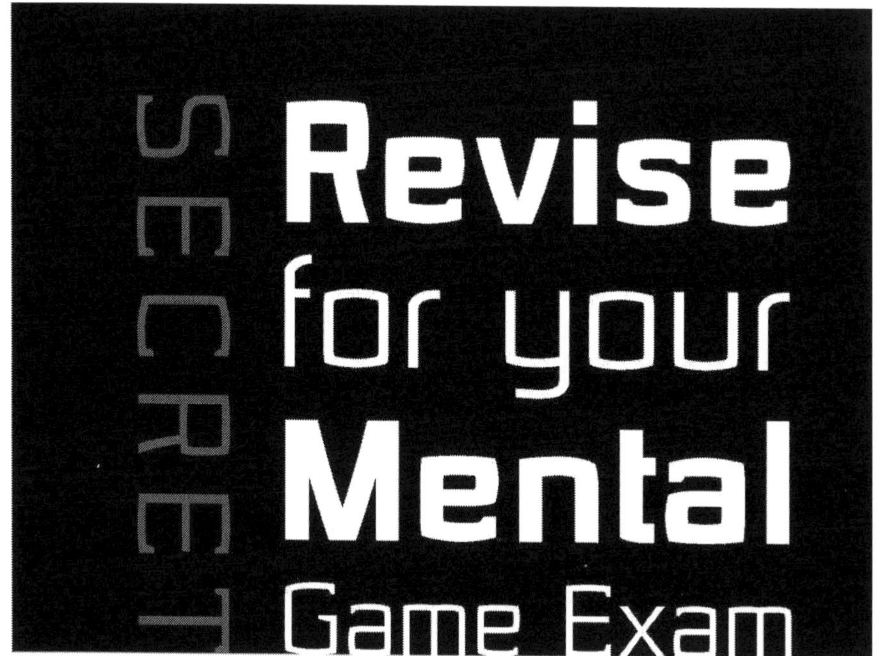
SECRET
Revise
for your
Mental
Game Exam

36

In order to do well in your school or college exams, you had to study hard and concentrate on the topics you thought would come up. You would have examined past papers, as they often provided a strong indication of possible questions, and then planned your revision around these predictions. By the time the exam would have come around, you'd have felt well-prepared, confident and ready to meet the challenge. More often than not, this intelligent approach to exam preparation would have led to good grades.

So, why not apply this methodical approach to your mental game preparation for competition? Spend some time identifying what's going to be asked of you and then prepare your responses in advance. In fact, this is something that world-class professional golfer, and multiple European Tour winner, Michael Hoey, engages in prior to tournaments.

Michael identifies the mentally challenging moments that tend to occur before, during and after his round, and translates these into a series of questions. You can see an example of his work below. Once his mental game questions have been isolated, Michael then plans and rehearses the best possible answers. These will involve many of the techniques found in this book.

MENTAL GAME QUESTION SHEET - *Michael Hoey*
1. *Okay Mike, you feel overly tense in the locker room. Five minutes to tee-off. A batch of unhelpful thoughts, images and memories have crept in uninvited. At this moment your mind is running away with things. You need to act quickly to regain control and reach your ideal performance state.* ***Can you do this? Now? How?***
2. *Observing the other two players in your three-ball, you notice their apparent ease as they approach the first tee. Suddenly you feel a sense of self-consciousness overwhelming you. You're annoyed by their apparent self-ease and poise. Where did this thought come from and, more importantly,* ***can you dismiss it right now? How are you going to do it?***
3. *While addressing the ball and going through your pre-shot routine on a short Par 5, your mind wanders off to the potential eagle on the hole and that the subsequent two shot gain would rocket you up to third on the leader board. This thought not only generates anxiety, but also takes your focus away from the job-at-hand.* ***What specific strategies will you use to reduce the over-arousal and regain your focus?***

4.	*You three-putt from a reasonable position on the green, and end up bogeying the hole. Frustration and anger besiege your mind as you walk to the next tee box.* ***How do you quell the angst and regain your composure? What specific techniques will you use?***
5.	*Between shots your thoughts drift off to the importance of this tournament to your season. All sorts of good and bad scenarios enter your mind and, in doing so, increase your arousal level, taking your attention away from what really matters - the next shot.* ***What's your technique for giving short shrift to your thoughts and for attending to the 'here-and-now'?***
6.	*You return to your hotel room. Unable to settle, your mind scans today's level par round, and before you know it you begin to beat yourself up for not doing better. You dissect the round and pinpoint errors. Your mood drops, you feel disconsolate, and you actually predict that you'll miss the cut.* ***What do you do? What's your response to this crucial moment?***

I strongly recommend that you see your mental game as an exam and revise for it. By transforming likely trigger situations into questions, just as Michael has shown you, you'll feel much more inclined to answer them. In this way, your mental preparation will be efficient and effective.

It'll be *efficient* because you will be targeting real things that could crop up in competition, rather than wasting energy on stuff that really doesn't matter and is not under your control anyway. And, it'll be *effective* since, by rehearsing mental techniques and strategies to deal with the specific situations, you'll be putting yourself right back in control of your performance. Your confidence will receive a major boost, a sense of mastery will emerge, and your chances of delivering a top performance will, without doubt, be greatly enhanced.

SECRET
Downward
Arrow
it

37

Many ill-prepared and average athletes believe they're demonstrating a positive mental attitude when they declare to all and sundry that they'll win their next match or competition. But they're fooling themselves, as saying it doesn't make it so. Winning requires much more than hot air and bravado.

It requires planning.

Top performers approach competition in a highly strategic way. While they want to win, their focus is on developing a process that maximises their chances of doing so. There's no hot air, just substance. Beginning with the end in mind (the win), they work backwards by asking penetrating and persistent questions to tease out what needs to be done. This is where the *Downward Arrow Technique* comes into its own. It enables the athlete or team to move from a desired outcome to the required process - from the 'what' to the 'how'.

A great example of this comes from my work with an Irish League team a few years ago. I was brought in to help the players from Larne FC prepare for one of the biggest games in their recent history. It was an Irish Cup semi-final against local rivals Ballymena United, managed at that time by the excellent Kenny Shiels, who went on to take charge of Kilmarnock in the Scottish Premiership.

Although Ballymena United were odds-on favourites to win the match, the bookies clearly hadn't allowed for the competitive edge that comes from a well-prepared team, a team that drilled deeply, who uncovered the 'how to' behind the yearned-for victory.

I began Larne's mental preparation by asking the team one simple question - *"Can you win the match?"* - to which there was a resounding, *"Of course we can!!"* As positive as this sounded, it didn't tell me much at all. I mean, was it confidence born out of evidence? Or was it bravado? Or, in fact, was it just out-and-out wishful thinking?

Taking things further, I used the downward arrow technique. The following exchange illustrates the technique's effectiveness in locating the 'how to' behind the Larne team's dream goal:

ME: "Okay guys, let's cut to the chase - can you win the match?"

Team: "Of course we can!!"

ME: "Great! And HOW are you going to do that? How are you going to win?"

Entire team: "Play better, play well, score more goals than them."

ME: "Okay. And HOW are you going to do that?"

Only two or three players: "Train well to make sure we play well."

ME: "Sounds good. But tell me how you'll do this? " [Pause]

One player: "It's about our jobs isn't it? It's what we do. And we must do it well."

ME: "Of course!" That's it. And HOW can you ensure this happens?"

Same player again: "We need to know our jobs, our roles on the park."

It was agreed that this was a good starting point for their preparation, and players, coaches and management agreed to meet up over the forthcoming days to nail down the specifics of each player's role.

These guys had never prepared with such depth and enthusiasm; a process which in itself raised confidence throughout the team. Nothing was going to be left to chance.

By adhering to a structured programme of technical and mental preparation, the players became steeped in their jobs. They knew what they had to do as individuals and, as a collective, fused into a self-contained, secure and committed unit. The signs were extremely promising. The so-called underdogs were going to bite back hard.

With the self-assurance that comes from rigorous groundwork, the Larne players took to the field on semi-final day determined to make the most of their opportunity, moment-by-moment, until the very last blow of the referee's whistle. And they did. They won the game 1-0. To a man, the team was superb, the performance outstanding. It was a great day all round.

And it should never be forgotten that the seeds of this success were sown in the previous days, and in the most innocuous of ways.

By a simple question, relentlessly pursued: "And *how* are you going to do that?"

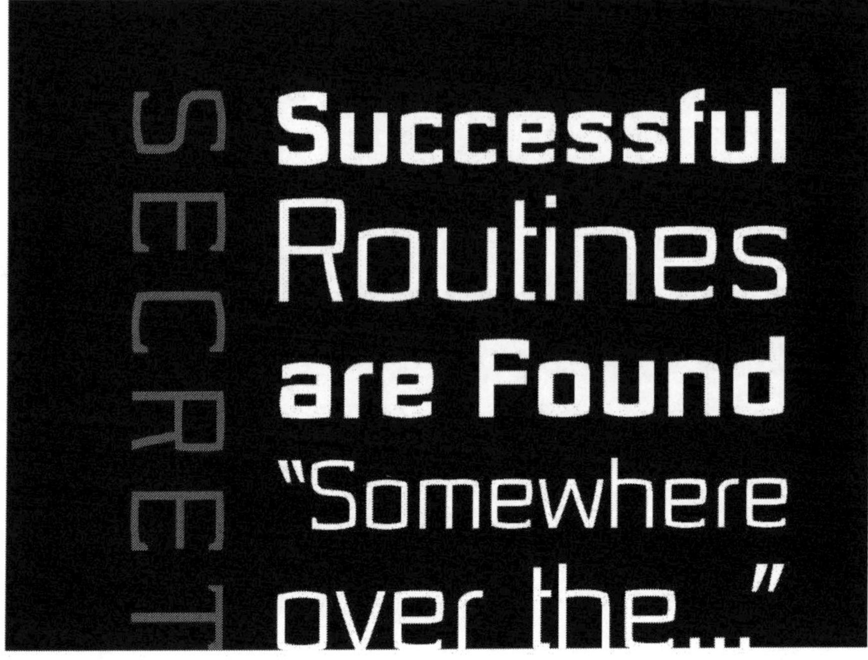
SECRET
Successful
Routines
are Found
"Somewhere
over the..."

38

You just couldn't help it, could you? The word RAINBOW just burst forth. Once you had read the three words 'Somewhere', 'Over' and 'The', in this exact order, you filled the gap in a nanosecond with the word 'Rainbow'. There was no conscious thought, as the classic song from the musical *The Wizard of Oz* has become so embedded in your mind. The movie has been on television so often that its signature song has become wired into your brain.

"Great", I hear you say, "but what on earth has the Wizard of Oz got to do with my performance?"

Well, almost everything. Especially, if you are

your team's penalty-taker or you play golf, or darts, or any sport where closed-skills are involved. To the armchair pundit, commentating from the comfort of his own home, a closed-skill situation looks simple: *"Just kick it through the posts for goodness sake. How hard can it be?!"*

Well, it can be really hard. Not the kick itself, but being able to quieten the mind to allow the kick to be executed smoothly and effectively, without the mental monster sticking its oar in. That's the hard bit, and it requires mental toughness. It requires routines that will lead the kicker to have full focus on the task in front of him. In other words, that leads him to *his* RAINBOW!

So, where Rainbow completed the sequence, *Somewhere*, *Over* and *The*, Full Focus can follow on from a similarly well-rehearsed routine. The key is to spend time designing such routines and rehearsing these, until they too stick in your brain. By taking certain steps, be they physical actions, reassuring verbal commands, or both, your brain can learn to complete the sequence with full focus on the job.

An athlete who finds his 'rainbow' time after time is Kevin Sinfield.

Sinfield, a professional rugby league player with Leeds Rhinos and captain of the England team, has become a sporting phenomenon, as his goal kicking is so incredibly accurate; the best in the Super League in fact. But as with all class acts, Sinfield's productivity is not by chance. It's the result of unstinting dedication to the art of goal kicking... and exploiting the human brain's hunger for routine.

Cut from the same cloth as David Beckham, Sinfield can be found alone on the practice pitch after training kicking ball-after-ball, honing his technique, broadbanding his brain for match day. Speaking to BBC Sport's George Riley, Sinfield describes his rigorous kicking routine:

> *"I use a telescopic tee with a bar in the middle which I use as my guide. I line it up pointed straight through the posts. I see the ball like a bullet. It has four panels. If you look at the end it is like a cross. So it is like looking down the barrel of a gun. I try and use that and use the lines on the ball as well as the line in the middle of the tee. For me, I place my middle finger on the valve of the ball. I line the seam of the ball up straight through the middle of the ball, knowing full well if I hit the bullet in the right spot it's going to go straight. You can have any run-up you want. Things to remember are relax, secondly keep your head down, and thirdly follow through. With my follow-through I try to touch my left hand with my right foot. I know if I hit the right spot, with the right follow-through, the ball will go straight and I don't have to look to see where it's going."* - BBC Sport, 02/05/13.

This is a wonderful illustration of how an elite athlete cultivates and employs an effective routine. I'm sure you'll agree that Sinfield's approach is meticulous. His attention to detail is fascinating and he fashions and embeds his routine by physically and mentally rehearsing it on a frequent basis.

It's this type of work ethic that sets the world-class apart from the ordinary. Are you up for it?

39

Those who excel in sport have strategies to deal with just about everything. So, as elite athletes expect to make errors every so often, they plan for these moments by having swift and effective routines to-hand.

These top performers understand that, when all is said and done, much of their success is down to how well they manage the tough moments during a performance. After all, it's really easy to manage the pleasant stuff. It just takes care of itself!

From over two decades of working with top athletes, I've found the best routines are those which obey what I call the 'A.I.M. Framework'. What this means, is that if you make a mistake, you need only do three things:

1. **A**cknowledge that the mistake has happened;
2. **I**mplement a technique that parks it in the past; and,
3. **M**ove on with your performance.

By taking A.I.M. you'll be able to move on quickly from those potentially distracting moments.

Now, as routines are like fingerprints, the one you design to help you move on from mistakes will be personal to you. Use the A.I.M. framework as a guide, and have a look below at the routine of a top European golfer I work with.

Potential Trigger
For the golfer, this could be an external event, such as a camera clicking or movement coming from the gallery of spectators. Or it could be an internal trigger, like thinking about the chances of making the cut, or winning the tournament, or dwelling on a poor start to the round. Whatever its origin, the distraction needs to be dealt with, and quickly.

So, the golfer takes A.I.M. in the following way:

Acknowledge. He recognises that he has become distracted. He names and claims it, and then does something about it.

Implement. He steps back from the moment, literally, and takes some deep breaths. The simplicity of this action is that it instantly brings his attention right back into the present. He also uses a verbal cue, "ENOUGH ALREADY", and a physical one - he brushes away his mental monster from his left shoulder, before then squashing the floored pest under his right golf shoe.

Move on. The moment he places his right foot on the ground, extinguishing the pest like a cigarette, he instantly shifts his focus to his next shot.

You can see how personal this golfer's routine is. By using the A.I.M. framework as a guide, he put his own signature on each of the three steps. Once designed, the routine was regularly rehearsed until he could traverse the three steps in a matter of seconds, and get on with his golf.

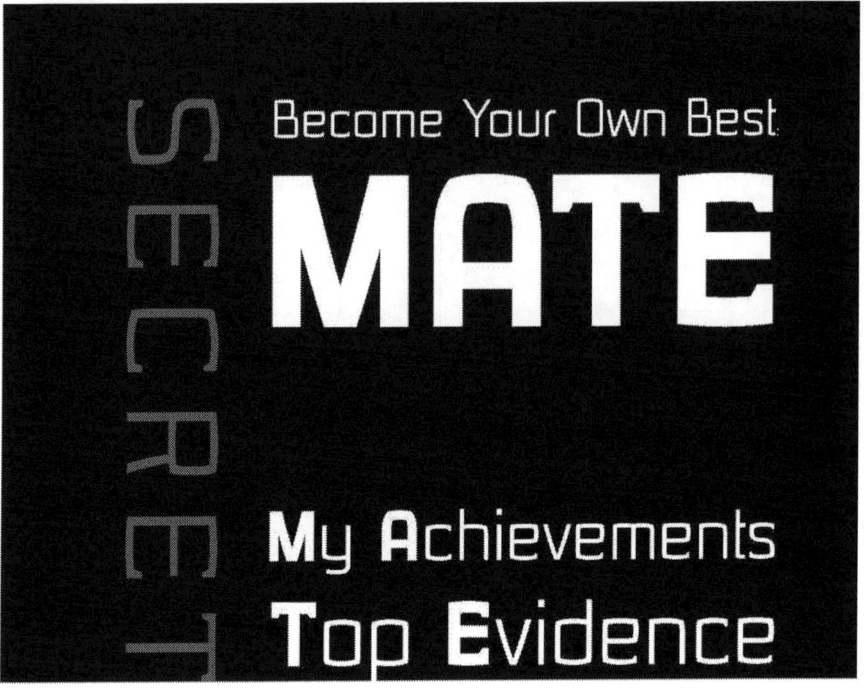

SECRET
Become Your Own Best
MATE
My Achievements
Top Evidence

Top athletes know themselves well, and are their own best friends. Realising that their outer world is a reflection of their internal one, they strive to feel comfortable in their own skin, and to like themselves, warts-and-all. They value, respect, and trust themselves, unconditionally.

It's from this polished inner core that great things spring forth. We're talking here about that much bandied about term *self-belief* - which encompasses two elements: self-esteem and self-confidence. The former is about how you view yourself as a person, while the latter concerns the degree to which you would back yourself to succeed in specific situations.

World-class athletes have high self-belief, an inner conviction that permits them to stride forward and make things happen. With faith in themselves, they accept who they are, and possess a cosy confidence in their ability to cope with particular challenges during performances.

Elite performers are not born with these qualities of course; none of us are. Rather they become evidence-gatherers and hoarders of self-supporting data. They know their weaknesses, but make a massive effort to bolster their strengths, and, with it, their self-belief. They use a range of strategies to do this.

And so can you.

Here's how, beginning with improving your **self-esteem**.

Start off by recording your accomplishments in life; not just from within sport, but across several areas. For example, you should look back over your education and employment experiences, your relationships, and, your spiritual side. Perhaps you have overcome a personal setback, or have helped someone else through troubled times.

Once listed, take each achievement in turn and identify what it must say about you; about your qualities as a person. Your courage, loyalty and honesty, for example. Or your ability to give and receive love. Perhaps they point to your capacity for working hard, or your perseverance and resilience in the face of adversity.

Whatever they are, note them down.

Don't be modest, as it's time to open up a *credit* account!

Once you have recorded your attributes, write them out onto crib cards and read them every day until they begin to sink in and replace all of the negative stuff you've accumulated about yourself, and that has devalued you as a person.

If you diligently follow this strategy, you'll experience a substantial lift in your self-esteem as you are identifying, appreciating and reinforcing your life achievements and accepting yourself unreservedly as a person of value.

The secret to building up world-class **self-confidence** is to exploit the link which exists between your memories, thoughts, images, emotions and your actions. When faced with specific challenges during competition, tough performers carry out mental activities that galvanise their sense of certainty to seal the deal, whatever the task may be. For a professional golfer the challenge could be a tricky, downhill, undulating putt to save par and to make the halfway cut in a big tournament. A top golfer I work with has faced this type of scenario on many occasions, and has developed a pre-shot regimen to increase his chances of success. Let's have a look at what he does. As he surveys his putt, he will:

- Recall his previous successes in similar situations.
- Act as if it is simply another shot, not a so-called 'crucial putt'.
- Take some soothing breaths to settle his nerves and centre him in the present.
- Complete his pre-putt routine to keep his mind focused on the process.
- Use vivid images to see and feel the ball take its path to the bottom of the cup.
- Have an 'I can do it' attitude
- Remove any fear by telling himself that he was made for such moments.
- Accept the outcome unconditionally.

The initial strand of this routine is key. A sense of having 'been there and done that' is a powerful boost to confidence. It takes the sting of fear out of the situation, offers reassurance, and generates the necessary focus and resolve to get the desired outcome.

One of my former clients, the now retired Scottish and Ulster rugby star, Simon Danielli, worked hard on nurturing his self-belief:

> *"I think key words pertaining to one's talents, and actual examples of these in past performances, are crucial for an athlete's self-perception and belief. I will often write down key words and examples of my best moments and this gives me confidence in the lead up to matches."* - Personal communication.

This secret is very clear about one thing - the world's most successful sports performers are continuously bolstering themselves. They give themselves credit for their achievements and are able to generate an inner conviction to help them deal with key moments during competition. By adhering to the maxim, '**M**y **A**chievements, **T**op **E**vidence', a great athlete is his own best mate.

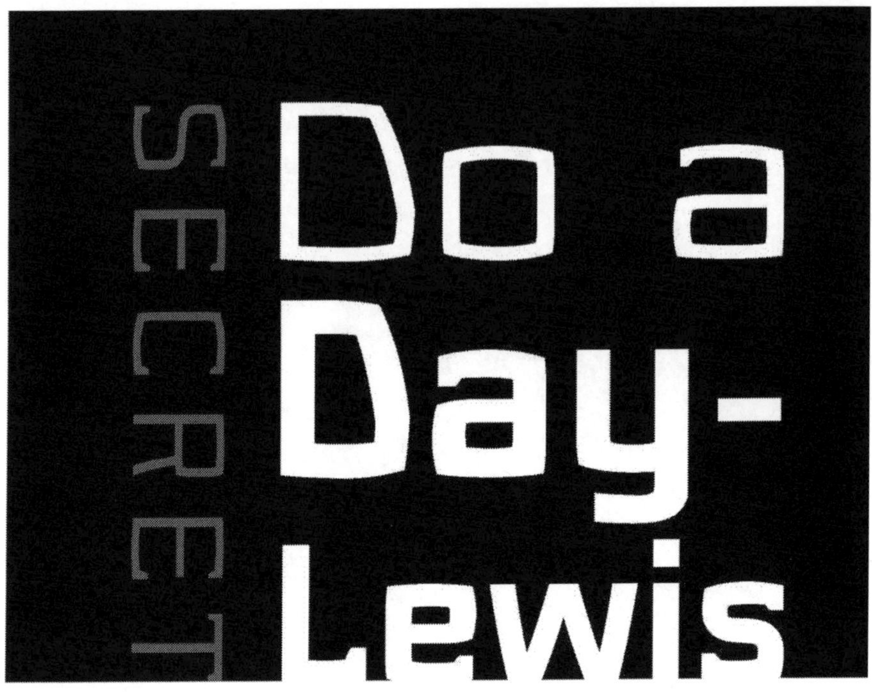

41

Multiple Oscar-winning actor, Daniel Day-Lewis, goes to extreme lengths to prepare for a part. This titan of stage and screen does all he can to get inside the mind and body of the character he's playing, and becomes this person, in all but genetics.

For instance, in the movie *My Left Foot*, where Day-Lewis portrayed Christy Brown, an Irish artist with cerebral palsy, he not only learned how to place a record on a turntable using his toes, but also stayed in character between takes. Remaining in his wheelchair throughout, he had members of the film crew feed him.

For the film *The Boxer*, he trained tirelessly

for eighteen months and became so skilled that his coach, former world champion Barry McGuigan, claimed that he was good enough to have turned professional. In his recent picture, *Lincoln*, he again remained in character between filming, with director Steven Spielberg claiming that he couldn't really see the join between actor and character. For all intents and purposes, Day-Lewis *was* Abraham Lincoln.

Surely Day-Lewis has discovered the nearest thing to cloning without DNA, or Dolly the sheep being involved!

While your preparation for competition is unlikely to demand such an extreme approach, the principles behind Day-Lewis' methodology shouldn't be ignored. Where an actor's job is to portray the attributes of a specific person, your role is to become the type of athlete you want to be.

For example, if you lack confidence, then you may want to research what this characteristic specifically means or looks like. You could begin by selecting a top athlete from your own sport who radiates self-confidence and study how he behaves. What is his posture like, particularly after a setback? Does he keep his head up and shoulders back? Does he smile in the face of adversity? What's he like during media interviews? Is he a modest sort of person in social situations?

In doing this bit of active research, you are in actual fact engaging in the preliminary stages of method acting. After all, you know the person you are to play (i.e. The Confident Athlete) and you have studied his mental and behavioural characteristics. The next stage then is to 'get into character', to act as if you already are 'The Confident Athlete'. It is important that you remain in character at every opportunity - in the manner of Mr. Day-Lewis - until your brain absorbs this new skill set. When you're no longer acting *as if* you're confident, but that you *are* confident.

It was American psychologist, William James, who identified the powerful reciprocal relationship that exists between body and mind. Used effectively, this partnership is the single greatest team in the universe. Think about it for a moment. You can improve the functioning of your body through mental training, and strengthen your mind through behavioural change. Two routes to self-improvement: mind to body, and body to mind.

Successful athletes develop their understanding of what it takes to become a champion by speaking to a champion; someone who has walked the walk. As such an opportunity is far too valuable to miss out on, you really should do all you can to make it happen.

Here are some guidelines to help you on your way:

42

- Begin by identifying the individual you'd truly love to chat to, and then make contact requesting a short meeting. The great advantage of the technological age we live in is that you can access contact details within minutes of starting your internet search.

- Write a sincere letter, or email, underlining the passion you have for your sport, and that in your pursuit of excellence you want to learn from the best. You will have your own way of wording this and capturing the reader's attention.
- Prepare thoroughly for the visit. Such privileged access may not come again. Have your questions at the ready, bring a notebook, or better still, ask if you could record the conversation.
- If you have difficulty arranging a face-to-face meeting, then you should consider emailing your questions to the individual. Perhaps a follow-up phone call or a chat on Skype could be arranged.

Just think what you could learn from this person; the information you could garner that will help you make progress in your sport. You could learn some tricks of the trade and powerful tips, and get a heads-up on some of the potential pitfalls.

Although your preference may be to meet up with a winner from within your own sport, you should broaden your focus to include champions from other sports, as well as elite performers from within the fields of entertainment and business. The secrets of success are largely the same, no matter where you look.

SECRET 43 Compassion Is not Just Something You Offer Other People

Unfortunately, one of our most highly developed skills is caustic self-criticism. Born out of the Frankenstein Factor, our capacity to rip ourselves apart and sabotage our efforts is off the scale.

You know what I'm talking about don't you? You make a mistake out on the pitch, court or course and before you know it you're engaged in a monstrous monologue of biting self-blame and name-calling. Left unchallenged, your inner critic will obliterate your performance, and restrict your career.

However, one of the most effective ways to disarm it is to use the power of self-compassion. For too long now, athletes have had a blind spot when it comes to being kind to themselves. It's seen as a soft and flaky self-indulgence, a weakening of the 'warrior' mindset.

Yet, the world's top performers are self-compassionate individuals, who have learned to cut themselves some slack during tough times. As far as they're concerned, inner kindness is not a feeble option at all, but a pragmatic and strong response to misfortune.

And here's why:

- Progress in sport, as in life, isn't played out in a linear fashion - each moment, performance, match, competition, day, month or year isn't always better than the previous one.
- We're all human, and there is no perfect.
- There are variables in life over which we have little or no control.

Self-compassion is a great mental tool and has a place in sport - because it works! Just because the macho world of sport barks out that self-kindness is for wimps, doesn't mean that you can't think for yourself and adopt a more reasonable approach to how you manage yourself and your failures.

Why not see your inner tormenter as someone to be pitied, a lost soul who really needs to grow up and not take his insecurities out on you? After all, this is the base from which all bullies operate. They are the ones with the problem. A bully is an energy vampire who lives off the distress of those whom he harasses, so it makes sense to cut off his energy supply by showing compassion. This allows you to take charge of the situation and regain the upper hand. This method works well whether the bully is your inner critic or your outer tormentor. Let me illustrate the former scenario with the case of *Sorrowful Sid*.

I have worked with 'Scott', a professional golfer, for a few years now, and like the majority of us he'd developed an inner bully. Indeed, this mental pest was so effective that Scott could turn an imperfect shot into a round- and tournament-busting *"tragedy"*. His reactions were often this unreasonable.

This young golfer needed to find a better way to manage poor shots, otherwise he was going to become depressed and possibly leave the sport altogether. Several methods were trialled, including the 'Inner Judge Judy' technique (Secret 21), but the one that worked best was compassion. Scott personified his inner bully as 'Sorrowful Sid' and began to treat this pest with sympathy.

In Scott's mind Sorrowful Sid had sad eyes, a scruffy appearance and a lonely existence; someone to be pitied rather than feared. From this piece of mental artwork alone, Scott began to feel a shift in the power balance, as his inner bully was no longer a big, powerful enemy. This technique worked a treat, as the very next time an unfavourable incident occurred during his performance Scott was able to shut Sid out:

> **Sorrowful Sid:** "You're absolutely useless. What sort of pathetic shot was that? And you call yourself a professional! If you can't even chip out of a bunker what chance do you have? And you're embarrassing yourself on television... "
>
> **Scott:** "Never you worry, Sid; I'll be okay. I know you can't cope with mistakes and feel you have to hit out at me and call me names. Hey, I understand this; you're scared of me failing. I get it, but that's enough now. I'm my own man and can cope with the odd poor shot and missed cut. So, ENOUGH Sid, I've a sand save to make!"
>
> **Sorrowful Sid:** "But..."

Scott: "That's ENOUGH now Sid. I've got this." [Takes a centred breath]

Sorrowful Sid: [SILENCE]

Scott has had great success with this approach, as self-compassion has largely silenced his inner bully. Sid has given up, as all bullies do, when starved of the expected reaction.

Sorrowful Sid joins 'Mournful Mervyn', another example from a professional athlete intent on silencing his inner critic through empathy and understanding.

You will have your own version, of course. You'll also need to prepare some *compassion scripts* so that your response to your inner critic is not only timely, but fluent. You don't want to be lost for words whenever it attacks. Record your compassionate responses onto cards and rehearse them until they become second nature.

Do not underestimate the power of compassion. Particularly when you apply it to yourself.

SECRET
Expecting Perfection
is a Most
Dangerous
Kind of
Madness

44

Here's the thing - if you *never* want to excel at anything, and to be dreadfully unhappy and unfulfilled to boot, then expect *perfection* in all that you do. Expecting perfection is one of the most brutal, self-inflicted strategies known to man and womankind. It will destroy your ingenuity, confidence and performance.

Perfection, of course, does not exist. So to expect it is, in the words of French dramatist Alfred de Musset, "*the most dangerous kind of madness.*" Yet many of us continue to expect the perfect performance, evening out, romantic encounter, wife, husband, son, daughter and death, for goodness sake. Not possible. Never was, nor ever will be.

If you expect to make no mistakes, and feel things should always go your way, then I've only one question to ask you: What on earth are you doing in sport? I mean, life must be tough enough for you, but sport, well, you'll be continuously dissatisfied, frustrated and, ironically, you'll frequently fail. You see, focusing on *not* making errors acts as a kind of mental magnet that actually makes their occurrence much more likely. (Also see Secret 49).

Unsurprisingly, the world's elite performers have sussed out this paradox. They have reassessed their ideas around success and set process and performance goals, which are largely under their control. They also develop what I call a 'preference-led' mindset. So, instead of demanding a perfect performance, top athletes give themselves permission to mess-up. Though naturally preferring not to make mistakes, they know that the secret is in *how* they respond to them when they do crop up, rather than in insisting they don't occur at all. Moreover, by accepting that they will make mistakes from time to time greatly reduces their anxiety and frees them up to play their game.

The real beauty of holding preferences is that they offer you psychological wiggle room. Where unmet demands often lead to harsh and distracting emotional reactions, such as anger and dejection, unmet preferences are generally interpreted much less severely, with the emotional fallout relatively low-key. At most a bit of disappointment or irritation may ensue.

Clearly, then, in mental game terms, having a *preference* to perform well in competition, is a superior approach to insisting that all goes swimmingly!

What I suggest you do now, is to revisit your expectations and screen them for signs of perfectionism. Are they realistic? If not, then you're setting yourself up for failure. Unrealistic expectations and perfectionism are first cousins. So look out for them.

Since perfection does not exist, you should adjust your goals to allow for the unanticipated, the unfavourable and the downright unfortunate. Ensure that your goals are under your control, as much as possible. To have 'Winning the Match' as your one and only goal is not useful at all, as winning is seldom under any athlete's full control.

The more realistic and flexible your approach, the more your performances will improve.

SECRET
Tackle
Team
Gremlin

In my first book, *Facing Frankenstein - Defeat Your True Opponent in Sport*, and from the secrets in this book, you know that your mental monster wants you to see the world in line with *its* agenda. It wants you to opt out of self-development and remain on the sofa. It abhors your notions of bettering yourself, as such activity brings with it the risk of failure, embarrassment and ridicule. As a result, it attacks your mind in the hope that you'll drop all those 'silly little thoughts' about being a sports superstar, or whatever.

45 Helping your monster to achieve this despicable goal is its private army, 'Team Gremlin'. These mental mercenaries infiltrate your belief system with distortions that will

negatively skew the ways in which you think about yourself and your ability to progress in sport.

Team Gremlin has six members, each a highly destructive thinking pattern in its own right, and each with its own role and responsibilities. Like any effective team, they work together to pack a powerful mental punch. Let's have a closer look at this mean team.

Gremlin 1: 'What if? /Ah, but' Thinking

This noxious gremlin seizes your in-the-moment focus and carries it away to the future. And not to a successful one at that. When this pest is in control, you'll find that your self-talk is heaving with worry:

- *"What if I make a mistake?"*
- *"What if I'm drawn against a lower ranked player and lose?"*
- *"What if it gets windy? I'm no good in tough conditions."*

This gremlin insists that you look for and find threat where little or none exists. And though you may try to reassure yourself that all will be well, it doesn't assuage your anxiety, as you soon retort with an *"Ah, but..."* and continue to worry. This thinking distortion will send your arousal level sky-high and affect all aspects of your performance.

Gremlin 2: Mental Filter

This is a particularly devious gremlin, whose sole role is to sabotage your confidence. It steers your attention away from the host of obvious positives in a performance and on to the one or two negatives. It's a nasty little pest capable of locating and dwelling on the one missed putt in a round of 65; the one bad training session in a week packed with great progress; and, the one piece of criticism within a chorus of congratulations.

Gremlin 3: Jumping to Conclusions

This mental gremlin wants you to form a pessimistic view of a situation, without having any facts whatsoever to support it. It will get you to engage in negative mind-reading and fortune-telling, hoping to make playing sport so uncomfortable for you, that you'll quit. You'll know this gremlin is doing its thing when you notice such self-talk as:

- *"After that display, the manager will think I'm a waste of space and drop me."*
- *"I just know that I'll not play well today. I just know it!"*

Gremlin 4: Rigid Reasoning

This gremlin will browbeat you into submission, by insisting that you set very stringent rules for yourself, other people and the world around you. These rigid beliefs can become so much part of you, that you'll often feel very upset whenever they're breached.

When this happens, you'll find that you attack yourself, and that shoulds, oughts and musts inhabit your self-talk:

- *"I shouldn't have missed that backhand."*
- *"I ought to be better than this."*
- *"I mustn't make another error."*

No pressure there then.

If left unchallenged, these types of negative interpretations will trigger emotionally unhelpful states, such as frustration, anger, anxiety and despair.

Gremlin 5: Over-Generalizing

This gremlin urges you to be melodramatic. When one negative event occurs, in one specific situation, it persuades you to generalise it to global proportions. Here the gremlin cuts out the middleman of reason and leaves you resigned to your fate. So, a golfer bogeys the first couple of holes and thinks to himself, *"That's it, I'll never win now."* A footballer is dropped from the team and makes the theatrical prediction that *"I'll never be picked again."* And a tennis player loses badly and claims, *"I'll always be second-rate. Everyone's better than me."*

You can catch this gremlin red-handed by noticing your use of the words: never, always, none, every, everyone, and no-one. You really must deal with this thinking distortion at the earliest possible moment, as it can trigger a self-fulfilling prophecy.

Gremlin 6: All or Nothing Thinking

This gremlin employs a good cop/bad cop routine to send you into an emotional tailspin. It persuades you to see life as either good or bad, positive or negative, black or white.

With judgements falling into only one of two camps, this thinking distortion places you in an awkward position. For example, if you underperform in competition, you'll be inclined to see yourself as a failure and, as a result, learn nothing useful from the contest. By writing your efforts off in such a dramatic way, you end up throwing the baby out with the bathwater, and miss out on the benefits to be had from a balanced performance review.

Given the potency of Team Gremlin, I urge you to be vigilant. These six bad boys lurk in the shadows of your mind, ready to strike at a moment's notice, particularly around competition time. Remember, they want you to remain in the narrowest of comfort zones and abandon any notion of making something of yourself.

So beware! These are horrible mental pests and you must fight them.

SECRET
Deal
With the
Destructive
Domino

46

'Deal with the Destructive Domino' is one of the most valuable mental game tools. Any technique that can save you a load of grief in competition, and turn your performance around in an instant, is worth its weight in gold.

The first step in developing this technique is to identify those times before, during and after your performances, when how you typically deal with certain incidents (e.g. errors, memory of errors, criticism, poor officiating) sets in motion a destructive domino effect. You know the type. It's not even a minute into your football match as a goalie and you mishandle a shot and concede a goal. Your lab rat response is to do what you've always done, and you beat yourself up with a biting *"I'm pathetic"*, and forecast that *"I'm going to have a nightmare in goals this afternoon."*

A mere sixty seconds in and you've pushed the first domino, which is the most destructive one. For it sets in motion a full-scale cascade of error-after-error, as your mind is not on the game, but instead focused on your poor play and what everyone watching must be thinking.

Now, it's important to stress at this point, that the first domino in the example is *not* your error on the pitch. Instead, it's your incredibly unhelpful and uncompassionate *response* to the error that triggers the domino effect. That's just the truth of it.

But there's another truth you must remember - YOU HAVE A CHOICE. You see, at the end of the day:

1. YOU have control over how you react to events.
2. YOU can learn to respond in a healthier and more constructive way to any set of circumstances.

By preparing better ways to manage such tough moments during your performance, you can stop the domino from falling. Do this and you have the opportunity to redeem yourself during the remainder of the contest.

Let's take a look at this technique in action with Ulster, Ireland and British and Irish Lions star, Rory Best. Rory approached me in 2005, when he was reserve hooker for Ulster, determined to take his mental game and performances to the next level. He wanted to be a regular on the Ulster team and to get an Ireland place. But his dream goal was to represent the Lions.

Within six months of our first meeting, Rory had not only become Ulster's number one hooker, but also made his debut for Ireland, against the All Blacks - and, as I write this book, he has captained the Lions during their tour of Australia.

This progress has been down to Rory himself, because, like all elite performers, he's motivated from within and is always looking for that edge, that something that'll make a positive difference, no matter how small the gain is. Many of these gains are to be found in the mental game, where a judicially used technique here, and a clever little strategy there, can make the difference between imploding and playing the game of your life.

One such strategy is the current one, and Rory has used it to great effect. By learning focusing skills and mistake-management routines, he is able to release his mind from errors and other potential distractions, and move on with his game. He has learned to avoid building the first domino. No first domino, no destructive domino effect.

Peter O'Reilly, of the Sunday Times, writing in December 2006, first noted Rory's capacity to get on with things: "*Rory Best doesn't seem to dwell at all on what's done, be it good or bad. He wants to know what's coming next.*"

Rory's ability to nail the first domino and to remain focused on the next task is brilliantly illustrated by his performance in a Heineken Cup game back in late 2005. The match against Saracens, at Ravenhill, was about fifteen minutes old, when Ulster had a lineout near to their own goal line. An overthrow by Rory was unfortunately intercepted by Saracens' lock Simon Raiwalui, who set up fly-half Glen Jackson to score the opening try of the game under the Ulster posts. You could see a domino coming.

But Rory dealt with the situation superbly. He stuck to his contingency plan, designed to manage such moments, and was able to accept the error and return his focus to the present. By locking back into the game, he remained in charge of what he did. He didn't yield to his mental monster, which would have urged him to topple over as many dominoes as it would take to get him back to the changing room for an early bath!

And guess what? Rory was rewarded for his mental strength.

With the match entering its closing minutes, and Ulster only two points up, Isaac Boss dissected the Sarries' defence with a grubber kick... and winning the rush to the line was Rory Best, who touched down with the decisive try of the game!

A great win for Ulster was settled by Rory at the end of the match. He'd sidestepped the destructive domino early on, stayed focused on his job and set in motion a positive chain reaction that lead to the winning try... and redemption!

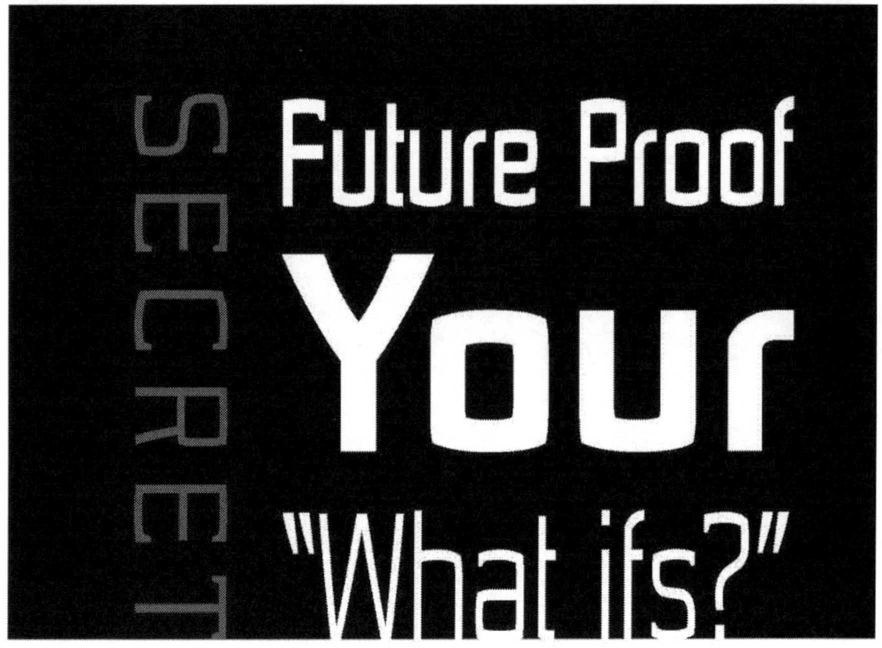
SECRET
Future Proof
Your
"What ifs?"

47

'What if?' thinking is a mental virus that, if left unchallenged, will overwhelm your preparation and performance. We are all familiar with this type of thinking:

- *"What if I forget my lines on the night of the play?"*
- *"What if she says no to a date?"*
- *"What if I make a mistake in front of the cameras?"*
- *"What if I'm substituted and lose my place on the team?"*

And so it goes on, and on and ON. And UNchallenged, most of the time. While we are adept at posing such unsettling questions, we are less proficient at answering the darn things.

Instead, we let them fester in some sort of suspended animation, poking away at our emotions , and keeping us in a heightened state of arousal and concern.

'What if?' thinking is totally self-created and only hurts the worrier. While the feared mistake is clearly yet to happen, the brain just doesn't see it like that. It responds to the worry RIGHT NOW. Which means that the worrier, by fretting over his future, destroys his present. For an athlete, this could result in a poor practice session, inadequate match preparation or underperformance.

You see, an unaddressed 'what if?' is regarded by the brain as a threat and, as a result, it will not release its focus on the worry until it is dealt with. That is why you really need to respond to each 'what if?' scenario quickly and constructively. Otherwise it will stalk you, in the same way that a brainteaser can torment you until it's solved.

I mean, have you ever gone to bed trying to remember the name of an actor in some movie? You know it, but simply can't bring it to mind, no matter how hard you try. Eventually you drift off to sleep, and then you wake up in the morning, turn to your startled partner, and say, *"Gregory Peck!! That's who it was!! He's the guy I couldn't remember!!"*

In this example, the brain trawled through its databank of memories during the night and answered the query. How great's that? But an important advantage for the Gregory Peck fan, was that the answer was already in storage and just needed to be retrieved. However, with 'what if?' queries, there's unlikely to be an 'off the peg' retort available in the system.

As a result, the worried mind darts about frantically looking for a solution. But with no answers available, the worry sticks, anxiety escalates and life begins to lose its shine.

So what do you do? Well, you need to actively respond to the 'what if?' with a rational counterargument. If we take one of the worries from the above list - *"What if I make a mistake in front of the cameras?"* - a useful comeback could be:

> *"Okay, fear of failure is common when playing in front of others. But it just means that the match is important to me. But, I draw the line at disturbing myself with such thinking and attracting the very thing I fear. Instead, I'll prepare for the possibility. This will give me confidence that I can cope, even if I do make a mistake."*

You cannot plan for every 'what if?' circumstance. However, at the very least, you should identify those scenarios that would, should they occur, throw a significant spanner in the works. These are personal to you of course. So fetch your jotter and pen and note down your most feared 'what if?' situations. Take each one in turn and devise strategies to deal with them.

Dealing with 'what ifs?' in this proactive way has two key benefits. Firstly, the act of preparing for the feared situation reduces your anxiety. And, secondly, if the situation does materialise, you can cope with it effectively.

Top class performers prepare for competition in the knowledge that a surprised athlete is an athlete in trouble. They realise that most of the things they fear are better prepared for than ignored, and that their future is largely shaped by what they do right now, in the present.

SECRET
Ticker-tape
Your
Thoughts

48

Many athletes get too caught up in their negative thinking and physical tension. For instance, they may actually question why they have negative thoughts in the first place (*"Why am I so keyed up today?"*) and how this must surely be a sign of a poor performance (*"There's no way I'll play well today feeling like this."*). And instead of simply disengaging from these thoughts, they do the exact opposite - they become far too involved in them, making them something they're not. So, rather than doing something much more productive, athletes end up adding extra layers of anxiety to their already anxious minds and sabotage their state of readiness for competition. Fortunately, there are two effective methods available to the sportsperson in the throes of such unhelpful thinking:

> **Method 1**. He can challenge his thoughts on the grounds of unreliable evidence and replace them with more constructive interpretations of the situation (as covered in Secrets 19, 20 and 21); or,
>
> **Method 2**. He can simply observe his thoughts and emotions, instead of engaging with them.

Method 2 is the 'Ticker-tape Technique', a much more passive, but equally effective alternative to challenging and changing unhelpful thinking (Method 1). It is used by many of the elite athletes I work with, who have been pleasantly surprised by its simplicity.

And it is simple.

The moment you catch yourself overanalysing a situation, with one anxious thought after another racing through your mind, take a few deep breaths, and imagine a blank screen in front of you. Now picture your thoughts gliding along the bottom of the screen, like the news ticker does on our 24 hour news channels. The latest share prices and news headlines just float on by, only to be observed, nothing more.

As Indian philosopher Ashvaghosha said: "*Thoughts of themselves have no substance; let them arise and pass away unheeded.*"

This exercise is only effective if you deliberately observe your thoughts, but don't engage with them. It's a bit like staring back at the school bully who expects you to cry, plead or run away.

A professional golfer I work with finds this technique extremely helpful, especially in those final minutes of preparation before his round begins; a time when he often becomes overwhelmed by intrusive thoughts. To ease the growing tension, he will take several abdominal breaths, and picture the blank screen in his mind's eye. Instead of observing his thoughts as a news ticker feed, he'll see them floating vertically up the screen and disappearing. He has become so good at this technique, that he can complete the task within a few seconds and reach his ideal state for tee-off.

Another one of my clients views his negative thoughts and feelings as pairs of animals wandering across his mental screen, as if headed for Noah's Ark. This is a particularly clever creation, as one animal in the duo represents the unhelpful thought, while the other symbolises the associated emotion.

The bottom-line with this technique, or any other presented in this book, is to do whatever it takes to make it work for you. I mean, if one of the top athletes in the British Isles can bring Noah and his Ark into his preparations, then I imagine anything goes!

So, be creative. It's your mind after all.

SECRET 49

Don't Think of George Clooney

(Now I said don't!)

This is what I asked the Northern Ireland Senior Women's football team to do. A simple enough request you'd think. Just don't think of George Clooney. How hard could it be?

Well, just about impossible actually, as the human brain cannot NOT think of something.

Try it. DON'T THINK of Gorgeous George, or Bootylicious Beyoncé. Or, any other person, place... or anything at all. Go on, don't think of it.

Incredible isn't it? You just can't do it. What's more, you end up doing the very thing you were aiming *not* to do! Your mind focuses on the person, place or thing.

Even Google can't compute a 'don't' instruction. Have a go. Google 'DON'T WANT WEBSITES OF MANCHESTER UNITED' and see what happens. You don't end up with a blank page. Instead, you're offered in the region of 470,000,000 results - just about half a billion pages more than you had requested!

Clearly then, an instruction containing a "Don't..." is counterproductive as it attracts the opposite of what's requested. If you're still unconvinced, then direct a "Don't run" at a group of galloping school children and see what happens. I rest my case.

So, having illustrated the paradox of a 'don't' instruction, courtesy of good old George, several of the Northern Ireland ladies conceded that they had a tendency to dwell on what they *didn't* want to happen in matches. Realising they could, unintentionally, be attracting the very things they feared, they took onboard my advice to flip their focus from 'don'ts' to 'dos'. In other words, to prepare for what they DO WANT TO HAPPEN during their performances.

This simple swivel in focus from negative to positive preparation is a distinguishing attribute of the mentally tough athlete. It's a shift in motivation from the avoidance of failure to the pursuit of success.

SECRET
Put a Lid
on the
Big Psych
Melting Pot
of Shame

In the summer of 2000, a self-appointed vigilante group attacked the home of a hospital paediatrician, after apparently confusing the doctor's professional title with the word "paedophile". It was a shocking case of misinformation creating misunderstanding.

Now, while a lot less serious, this phenomenon is also alive and well within the public's view of psychology.

In the same way as the above group saw the prefix 'paed' and reacted to it as if in full possession of the facts, society frequently sees the prefix 'psych' and envisages all sorts of associated negatives. It seems that all things *psych* are thrown into a big communal pot, casserole style, before being well-stirred by rumour, seasoned with media images, brought to the boil by downright prejudice, and served with shame. After consumption, the taste left in society's mouth from supping at the Big Psych Melting Pot, is a belief that it knows exactly what psychology is; and often not in a good way.

Of course, as athletes are part and parcel of our society, we shouldn't be surprised at all that they too have supped from this melting pot, and gained a bellyful of *psych* prejudice. Accordingly, many athletes hold preconceptions about psychology in general, along with an unhealthy side order related specifically to sport psychology itself. Here are a few examples:

- Consulting a sport psychologist is a sign of mental weakness.
- Seeing a sport psychologist means you'll be labelled as mentally ill.
- Sport psychology can't alter what you've been born with psychologically. You're either mentally tough or you aren't. It can't be learned.
- Sport psychologists control athletes' performances through hypnosis.
- Working with a sport psychologist leads to an overreliance on the practitioner.
- Sport psychology is only for top athletes.
- Sport psychology can quickly fix performance problems.
- Sport psychology is like psychotherapy.

These fears and misunderstandings come out of the Big Pot, and create caginess in athletes about seeking guidance from a sport psychologist. This is unfortunate and goes a long way to explaining what I call 'The Mental Game Conundrum'.

Bring together any group of athletes and coaches and they will, almost to a man and woman, agree that the mental side of sport is crucial to performance excellence. Yet, proceed to ask the very same group "How many of you engage in regular mental skills training?" and you will be met with, at best, a smattering of affirmative responses.

It's the case, then, that many athletes continue to dodge the sport psychologist in the same way many of us in a packed Pharmacy would shirk the chemist's strident appeal, "haemorrhoid cream; who ordered the haemorrhoid cream?" How many of us would stride up to the counter, head in the air, and announce "Thank you Madame, I am indeed the rectally-wrecked one and am terribly grateful for your tube of soothing lotion... No need for a bag, I'll apply it here."?!

Not one of us I would say.

We'd be more inclined to turn our heels and run (well limp) for it, sacrificing healing on the altar of shame and stigma.

It's this self-defeating mindset that prevents some athletes from ever becoming elite performers. They end up forfeiting mental toughness, peak performance and career development, because fighting through the perceived stigma about seeing a sport psychologist is too much hassle. Too uncomfortable.

Instead they make do, while the truly ambitious performer trains his mind as well as his body.

So, how ambitious are you?

What a shallow bunch we really are!

When we meet people for the first time, do we ever ask them about their current state of happiness? No, we don't!

Rather, we go straight for their achievements: *"So, what do you do?"; "Where do you work?"; "What do you drive?"; "Where do you live?"; "Did you go to university?"; "What degree did you get?"; "Married?"; "Do you have kids?"; "Are you going to have more kids?"; "What school does your daughter go to?"; "Is she in the top stream?"; "What does she want to be?"; "Does she play an instrument?"; "What grade has she reached in piano?".*

And so on and so forth. From birth to death it

is about outcomes. At birth: *"I know he's only five hours old, but are you going to put Tristan's name down for Prep School?"* At death: *"Old Tristan would have loved the way the vicar read out all of his qualifications. The classiest funeral I've ever been at!"*

These examples are not that farfetched at all. I've witnessed many a conversational egofest where participants are eager to outdo one another. I'm sure you've seen this type of one-upmanship from approval junkies.

To be fair, many of us have been moulded from an early age to obsess about our place in the pecking order of life. To fixate on our status, real or perceived, and to worry about what other people are doing and achieving. When all is said and done, we have been indoctrinated into what I call the 'Cult of Results'.

Devotees of this cult set themselves up for failure. By focusing far too heavily on the prize, they distract themselves from the very process that could've led them to it.

You can overcome the cult's brainwashing by:

- Recognising that you have indeed been conditioned to think in certain unhelpful ways.
- Understanding that it's not about the pursuit of your success, but the success of your pursuit.
- Refocusing on your achievement plan and enjoying the journey of attaining big goals.
- Igniting your inner spark by staying with the process of achievement.

By adhering to these four principles you will not only begin to think and focus like a top class athlete, but your competitive performances will also start to show significant improvement.

SECRET
Reignite Your
Childhood
Appetite for
Placing Your Mind in
Exciting Places

52

Looking back over the years, you'll find that your imagination was yours up to about the age of ten. At this point, the left-brain-dominated education system began to ratchet-up its influence, and year-after-year you became increasingly proficient at thinking and analysing. The occasional break from left-brain pummelling came during those classes when your creativity was given some air - in art class, for instance. But these were rare moments. So much so, that right-brain people have become objects of ridicule and are often seen as strange, 'arty' types.

This change from in-the-moment creative child, to thinking machine, only took a few years. And, while learning how to think and analyse is clearly useful, it should never have been at the expense of our ingenious right brain. But it was.

Our education was a game of *one* half.

By neglecting the beautiful, limitless right brain, our schooling has essentially firewalled us off from being able to live more fully in the present. Our creativity and our ability to imagine have been stymied. And for the budding athlete the power of the imagination is absolutely crucial to his sporting success.

As you would expect, the world-class refuse to accept this imposed restriction and instead work hard to rekindle their childhood capacity for taking their minds to exciting places. By taking back control of their imagination, these athletes, in effect, harness the ability to prepare in the most effective way possible, and to perform with greater confidence, focus and fluidity.

It would be foolish to ignore imagery. It is an incredible facility that creates REAL change in your brain, as your neurology is stirred by vivid images in the very same way that the actual physical activity would stimulate it:

> "*Connections among neurons can be physically modified through mental training just as biceps can be modified by physical training.*" - Prof. Richard Davidson, University of Wisconsin-Madison.

Wow! How great is this? You can practice your technical skills from home! It also explains why top athletes have learned to profit from this most amazing of human gifts - the capacity to imagine. I believe that author, Michael Cibenko, was right when he said that "*what we sometimes call 'genius' is simply a refusal to altogether let go of childhood imagination.*"

SECRET
Exploit Your
Mental
Swiss
Army Knife

53

As a mental game tool, imagery (also known as visualisation and mental rehearsal) involves the harnessing of the human ability to create mental movies. Multi-dimensional movies of the mind, shot in glorious technicolour, with Dolby Surround Sound, and directed by the most sophisticated of remote controls - free will. For you the athlete, imagery is your flexible friend. It is incredibly versatile, only limited by your creativity, and has multiple uses across the performance cycle. It's your own mental Swiss Army knife!

Before competition, you can use imagery to:

- Rehearse and consolidate your skill sets, game strategy, tactics, contingency plans and routines.

- Increase your motivation and commitment to training and performance.
- Speed up the learning, acquisition and proficiency of your technical skills.
- See, feel and otherwise sense peak performance and success.
- Gain mastery over key situations ahead of time.
- Boost your arousal level.
- Relax an overactive, anxious mind and tense body.

Former Ulster and Scotland rugby wing, Simon Danielli, gained a lot from using imagery as part of his pre-match preparations. He was able to place his mind in the various situations that would arise during games and ready himself for those 'what if?' scenarios. This instilled him with confidence, as he knew he could deal effectively with whatever cropped up and still go on to deliver a high level performance.

> *"In a game of so many variables like rugby, as in most sports, many scenarios are going to be presented throughout the match. Knowing that you can cope with them and that you have the tools to deal with or exploit them is so important. How players arrive at this knowledge is totally individual, but many players like to visualise scenarios, many of which they have encountered in recent games and performed successfully. I like to play over a few of my 'best moments' in my head before games."* - Simon Danielli, Personal communication.

Former WBA World Super Middleweight boxing champion, Brian Magee, knows that when he leads with his mind, his body follows. Knowing that excellence doesn't happen by chance, he is meticulous in his mental preparation for fights, with imagery a vital pre-fight tool. Brian rehearses his fight plan, tactics and strategies, and places himself in the fight, seeing himself performing at his best. Moreover, he mentally inoculates himself against the jolt of the unfamiliar. By visiting the arena ahead of time, watching DVDs of previous fight nights, walking the walk from locker room to ring, he deposits in his memory bank crucial information ripe for imagery.

> *"[Imagery] is the most important tool for me, as it familiarises me with my opponent, for example seeing myself fight him in the arena. If I've never been there before [imagery] limits the amount of surprises or upsets you have to deal with up to and during the event. If you have imagined it, it's already happened. You've dealt with it and most important you did it with a positive outcome for yourself."* - Brian Magee, Personal communication.

During the performance itself, imagery can enable you to:

- Rehearse a distinct, closed-skill right before its execution. For instance, immediately prior to: lineout throws (rugby union); free/penalty kicks (football); free-throws (basketball); serving (tennis, squash); and, all golf shots.
  For Ulster, Ireland and Lions rugby hooker Rory Best, imagery is an essential component of his pre-throw routine:

  > *"I would be visualising the point, closing my eyes and trying to picture where the ball is going. Whenever the call comes in, I'll get myself ready and bring the ball back. I'll see that target in my head a split second before I throw it so I'll know where I am putting it."* - www.irishrugby.ie.

- Positively reinforce a great piece of play. After a well-executed skill, you can anchor it in your brain by running it quickly through your mind. This is a strong hint for your brain to repeat it under similar conditions.

- 'Rub out' and 'record over' an error with the correct execution of the skill. This need only take a second or two and will reassure your mind that all is well and that it's time to get on with the game.

After competition, you can use imagery to:

- Review your display. As your very own *iPlayer*, imagery can supply you with performance highlights - you can run and rerun instances of excellence through your mind. This will enhance your mood and confidence and direct your brain to repeat these great skills next time.
- Learn and move on from the bad bits. Here you can use imagery to replay the less pleasing aspects of your performance, to understand why they occurred and to then 'tape' over them with the preferred version. Ulster, Ireland and Lions winger Tommy Bowe uses imagery in this way:

  "In sport, most people have felt what defeat is like. It is very important to find out what went wrong early and move on. I try to see where I went wrong, then visualize doing it right and put it out of my mind then." - Tommy Bowe, Personal communication.

- Assist your recovery from injury. It can help to speed up the healing process, aid pain management, and provide a means of rehearsing your return to competition.

Imagery really is this versatile. Used effectively, its reach extends right the way through your mental game, strengthening it in many ways as it goes.

SECRET
C.R.E.A.T.E.
the Blueprint For
Peak
Performance

54

It was comedian, George Carlin, who observed that "*Electricity is really just organized lightning.*" Well imagery, as a mental game technique, is really just organised imagination.

Imagery is seeing and sensing things, people or scenarios in the mind. Have a go. Pick an object from your sport, a piece of equipment or team badge for instance, and see it in your mind's eye in as much detail as possible. Perhaps you can almost feel it, as the item has been part of your life for many years.

How did it go? I'm sure you did a good job. Now, carrying out this type of exercise is not a million miles from using imagery as a mental game tool. It just requires a systematic approach, plenty of practice, and a plan of when and where to apply it across the performance cycle.

To help you on your way, you should follow the C.R.E.A.T.E. training system. This method sets out the six key principles of effective imagery:

- **C**lear the Canvas
- **R**ealistic
- **E**nduring Practice
- **A**ssimilate
- **T**op-Up
- **E**valuate

Clear the Canvas

As imagery exploits the mind-body relationship, it is really important that the channel of communication between the two is free from interference. Remember, you are aiming to reproduce specific scenarios in your mind, so that you can rehearse these away from the training ground. As you want your brain to perceive these situations as 'real', it stands to reason that you'll need to generate brilliant and vibrant images. And you'll be better placed to do so, if you start your session with a short relaxation exercise (see Secret 30). This will quieten the mind, clear the canvas for your imagery, and boost the signal from mind-to-body.

Realistic

Your imagery needs to be an authentic depiction of the selected scenario. To more accurately match reality, you should run your imagined scenes in real time and make sure to incorporate as many of your senses as possible. After all, when you compete in your sport, it's not just a visual experience. There will also be kinaesthetic, aural and olfactive aspects to it. By bringing in these senses, you will begin to feel you are actually 'there', in the imagined scene, and accordingly the communication between brain and body will be at its sharpest.

This is a technique recognised by Raj Koothrappali from the wonderful US comedy show, *The Big Bang Theory.* In a credibility-saving, let's-get-our-story-straight debate with friend Howard Wolowitz (after they had failed to attract a couple of Goth girls during a night out clubbing), Raj ensures that their fabricated story feels as genuine to him as possible:

> "**Howard:** *Okay, wait, how about this? We say there were four Goth girls, the two girls in the club had two friends.*
>
> **Raj:** *I like it, I like it. Did they smell good despite their gothlike nature?*
>
> **Howard:** *What's that got to do with the story?*
>
> **Raj:** *Engaging my olfactory sense helps make it real for me.*
>
> **Howard:** *Fine, they smelled good.*
>
> **Raj:** *Oh, they did. Like jasmine and honeysuckle.*
>
> **Howard:** *Whatever!"* - 'The Gothowitz Deviation', Season 3, Episode 3.

Clearly, your imagery will be positive. You'll see yourself mastering situations and performing skills with excellence. This can be done from either an internal or external perspective. When you adopt an internal or first person perspective, you are *in* the imagined situation, performing, say, a specific skill set, and seeing and sensing the activity as you would in reality. The advantage here is that you can match up the virtual world with the real world. This is a fantastic method of preparation.

Imagery generated from an external viewpoint is like watching yourself on a movie screen. This approach is especially useful when you need to observe and assess aspects of a particular technique.

Enduring Practice

If you really want to profit from using imagery, then you need to engage in regular, quality practice. There are no shortcuts. Practice should initially be on a daily basis, and you should prepare for each session. Decide on the situations to be rehearsed and allocate around four minutes per session, particularly over the early stages. It is tiring work and it's best to build things up gradually over time. It is important to set goals, otherwise it'll be just about impossible to evaluate your progress in a meaningful way.

Assimilate

Make sure your imagery practice and real world practice have a mutually beneficial relationship. For example, if you execute a skill sublimely in training, you should replay it in your mind as soon as you can, thereby lodging it in your imagery bank for future reference. This is an example of the real world informing your virtual world. The converse should happen too - imagery should be used in preparation for a training session.

You may, for instance, engage in some rousing imagery to elevate a low mood prior to a rigorous weights session. Or, perhaps, you'll raise your motivational pulse by using imagery to remind yourself of your dream goal and that the hard yards will be worth it.

Top-Up

As you become more skilled in your sport and accumulate new experiences, you should update the content of your imagery. Ask yourself if there are any changes in what it looks and feels like to play your sport; even in how it now sounds or smells! Any changes, no matter how subtle, should be incorporated into your imagery sessions in order to keep it real.

Evaluate

When developing any skill in life, it is always good practice to assess how things are going. And it's no different with imagery. As the Steven Spielberg of your mental movies, it is your job to evaluate how good they are and if they are fit for purpose. To do this, you should consider the:

- Effectiveness of your pre-imagery relaxation technique.
- Level to which you incorporated all of your senses.
- Degree to which you felt at-one with the imagined scenario.
- Extent of control you had over the images.

Use a simple 10-point rating scale to assess your proficiency across these elements.

I cannot encourage you enough to work hard at mastering this valuable mental game technique. Make it an integral part of your preparation and use it strategically during and after competition. Imagery 'burns' success into your neurology and will help you move from virtual winner to a champion in real life.

SECRET
Hold
Mini
Tutorials

How do you know if you've really grasped a particular subject or technique?

I certainly remember several occasions at school when I'd leave a class feeling sure I'd understood the topic being taught. Similarly, I could read an important part of a textbook and feel that I had absorbed the knowledge. But when I was tested, it turned out that I knew much less than I thought!

55 So what on earth was going on? How could I feel so self-assured, and then bomb-out in such a fashion?

Well, I'd been engaging in that age-old human activity, self-delusion. I had fallen for the illusion that feelings equated with facts.

Because I *felt* I knew my stuff, I assumed I actually did!

From time to time we all fool ourselves that we're on top of things, when we're not. However, those who attain success in any field, approach the learning process in a much more robust way. They strip away any chance of self-deception, and expose the raw nerve of the truth. To test their understanding of an important aspect of their discipline, the best do what many of their rivals would fear to do - they TEACH the topic to others.

By doing this, they place themselves in a very strong position, as they'll be left in no doubt whatsoever about how well they know their stuff. Their 'pupils' will see to that.

Teaching a topic forces you to go deep, as Daniel Coyle (author of *The Talent Code*) might put it. To carry it off effectively, you will need to prepare in a purposeful way, and know the subject to such a degree that you can respond positively to the inevitable questions that will come from the floor. In fact, it's this very part of the teaching experience that lets you know just how much you know.

If one of the secrets of effective learning is *to teach the topic*, then how can you apply this principle to mental toughness training for sport? Well, I suggest you select a specific technique, like imagery, and study and practice it thoroughly, before then holding a mini tutorial with a small group of enthusiastic learners. These could be friends or family members, teammates, or, if you're really up for the challenge, a group of bona fide students on a sport psychology course. It's extremely important to set some learning objectives to help structure your preparation and to evaluate the effectiveness of your teaching.

If we take imagery as the selected technique, then you could inform your trainees that, by the end of the tutorial, they should have a basic understanding of: what imagery is; how it works; its benefits; when it can be used; and, how to apply it. You should also encourage questions, remembering all the time that the ultimate student in this exercise is YOU.

The TEACH IT approach will help take your mental game to the next level and beyond. I suggest you apply the method to some of your favourite secrets in this book. In this way, you will be following the lead of some of the world's most successful sportspeople who consolidate their learning by tutoring others.

SECRET Choose to Snooze It's the Nap Selection

The best performers in world sport, and those aspiring to join them, search for strategies and ideas that will deliver even a fractional gain. While their rivals turn their noses up at strange or silly sounding interventions, the world's best remain open-minded. They will research the idea, and come to an informed decision as to whether or not to pursue it. If anything useful can be achieved - no matter how small the gain - then they are liable to give the suggested intervention a go.

One such suggestion is to see a Sleep Coach. Yes, they do exist. And Nick Littlehales is one of the best. Littlehales' client list is a who's who of the sporting world. From advising the superteams of Arsenal, Liverpool and

Manchester United in the English Premier League, to guiding the cyclists of Team GB, the man known as the Sports Sleep Coach has helped many top athletes master the art of getting great sleep.

It's surely of little surprise that living legends, Sirs Chris Hoy and Bradley Wiggins of the cycling world, have consulted Littlehales for advice. Attention to detail is what these guys are all about. If a performance advantage can materialise from learning how to sleep properly, then it will be learned. After all, it could be the fractional gain that leads to a fractional win - by half the width of a bicycle tyre, for instance.

> *"Britain's cyclists do not do anything as prosaic as going to bed, perchance to dream. They go there to win, on personalised pillows and layered memory-foam mattresses covered by hypo-allergenic sheets. Lighting, and the quality of air flow, is strictly controlled as they sleep. The unique beds, the product of a partnership with sleep coach Nick Littlehales, were installed in the Olympic Village this month. Welcome to Dave Brailsford's (performance director) world, where the search for fractional advantage is a 24/7 business."*
>
> - Michael Calvin, Independent on Sunday, 29/07/12.

Littlehales claims that when we awaken, we should feel rested and ready to rumble; which of course sounds like an obvious goal. Yet my guess is that the majority of us wake up tired; often just as tired as when we went to bed. Which is never a good start to any day, is it? And for the athlete, it can have an increasingly adverse impact upon his performance over time.

In view of this, it would be entirely sensible for any ambitious athlete to follow Littlehales' detailed guidance around improving the sleeping environment.

Littlehales stresses *quality* - quality preparation and quality accessories (from mattresses to dawn simulators) - while research in the field of revitalising sleep also points to the need for *quantity*. Cheri Mah, a scientist with the Stanford Sleep Disorder Clinic, found that the performances of elite basketball players improved by increasing their hours of sleep, by almost two hours per night, to ten hours. This 'sleep extension', when compared to baseline readings, accounted for improvements in the players' sprinting speeds (by 5%); shooting accuracy (by 9%); reflexes; alertness; and, mood. Ten was the magic number with these players, so much so, that if their travel demands got in the way of reaching this quota, they took naps during the day to compensate. The athletes also refrained from drinking coffee and alcohol.

Findings similar to these have been found across other sports, including swimming, football, tennis, golf and athletics. Increase your hours of sleep and you will enhance your athletic performance. However, such improvement is a gradual affair - one good night's sleep will do little in the long-term to sharpen your competitive edge. Instead, you should integrate a robust sleep routine into your training and competition schedule for the entire season. A neat way to think about this is to see this new regimen as a type of repayment plan, one designed to wipe out what experts call *sleep debt*. And I have to say, many of us are in arrears.

By accumulating night-upon-night of inadequate rest, our sleep debt starts to spiral out of control, with inevitable and negative consequences on our energy levels, decision-making, reaction times, cognitive functioning, temperament, performance/productivity, and physical recovery and repair.

Sleep is also the time when the brain grows new cells and consolidates what is called 'procedural memory', which is used to embed skills. When we're learning a specific technique - for example, a golf shot, free throw, or tennis serve - we need our brain to really grasp what it feels like to execute the moves, an understanding that is reinforced during sleep. Here the procedural memory is encoded, with the brain establishing the connections responsible for performing the skill. Dr. Matthew Edlund, Director of the Centre for Circadian Medicine in Florida, describes this process in a powerful way:

> "*In sleep, we grow new brain cells. In sleep we lie down and rewire memories. No sleep, no new brain cells. And our reworked brains are literally different when we wake up, sort of like those science fiction stories where people awaken each day a whole new person. Every night we have rewired, rebuilt, reset, reconstructed, and redone our brains.*"

Earlier in the book, you were introduced to deep practice and discovered how it broadbands the brain for excellence (Secret 12). Well, now you know that the broadbanding is consolidated during great sleep.

It is of utmost importance that you treat rest and sleep with respect. Design a routine that fits in with your life, one that allows you to increase your hours asleep, and to incorporate many of the quality features highlighted by Littlehales.

As a final point, I think we can now safely consign the late Margaret Thatcher's 'Sleep Is For Wimps' aphorism to the dustbin of 80's swagger. For the truth is this: SLEEP IS FOR WINNERS.

SECRET
Get Connected to the
Grid
of Life

The world's top athletes see sport as one element of their lives, albeit an important one. They see themselves as more than footballers, golfers, rugby players, cricketers or sprinters. They are fathers and mothers, brothers and sisters, sons and daughters. Some are aunties, uncles, friends, colleagues, lovers and partners, as well as churchgoers, musicians, artists and students.

57

These athletes have learned that living a life of wall-to-wall training and competing is no life at all, and what's more, is a recipe for physical and psychological burnout. They realise that more isn't always better, and that when it comes to practice, quality trumps quantity.

By developing a strong social network and interests outside sport, they create a balance in their lives that's eventually reflected on the inside. Getting away from it all, even in short bursts, helps to recharge their energy levels by refreshing mind, body and spirit. This balance also means they don't put all of their self-esteem eggs into the sporting basket, and thus avoid linking their emotional wellbeing to their results. They know that such rigidity would only lead to bouts of extreme frustration, deflation and low self-worth.

What about you? Have you a healthy sport-life balance? Or do you believe you must never let your guard down, let alone your hair, otherwise failure will ensue? Consider these questions, be very honest with yourself, and if changes are required to bring a bit of equilibrium back into your life, then make them.

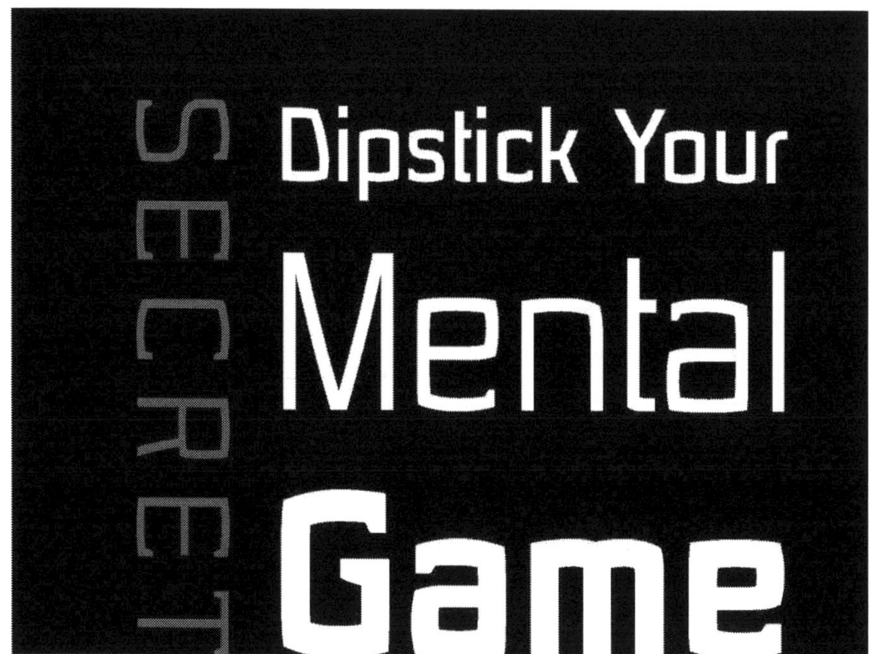
SECRET
Dipstick Your
Mental
Game

Without a strong mental approach to your sport, you are behaving like the motorist who believes that oil isn't really that big a deal. As a result, he hardly ever checks the level in the tank, and only deals with it when the dashboard light tells him to. This casual and irresponsible approach means he risks the performance and longevity of his very expensive car; a prized possession (though clearly not prized enough), that may have taken him years to save for.

58 Unfortunately, many athletes have a similar attitude to the oil that runs their physical machinery, only attending to their mental game when the warning light of a performance slump can no longer be ignored. All of a

sudden, they see the importance of their minds in the effective running of their bodies, and realise that the months and years of physical and technical training could be seriously compromised by their untrained brain.

While they may outwardly appear to be the Ferrari of the sporting world, without the lubricant of self-belief, motivation, focus and composure, they will simply not make it. Instead, their hopes, goals and careers will be abandoned on the hard shoulder of progress, while those who train their brains speed on by.

If you are serious about your sport, and want your performance to purr, then you must check your levels of mental strength on a regular basis. To do this, you need to dipstick your inner game. In fact, have a go right now. Fetch a pen and paper and record your responses to the following questions:

- Are you self-motivated? Do you set personally challenging goals and have a plan to achieve them? Or are you a bit too casual about your direction of travel?
- Do you worry far too much about what other people are thinking? In fact, are you, for the most part, competing to please others and to gain social approval, status and acceptance? Or for material gain?
- Do you know your Personal Ideal Performance State (PIPS)? If you do, can you regulate your arousal to reach your PIPS prior to competition? Or do you tend to reach this state by chance, and therefore it's not under your control? (See Secrets 28 and 29).
- Are you able to remain composed during competition? Or are you prone to irritation, frustration, worry or rage?
- Do you feel controlled by events around you? When you make a mistake, for instance, do you believe that it 'causes'

your anger, embarrassment or anxiety? Or are you able to interpret such events in ways that help you to stay composed and focused?

- Are you able to concentrate on what matters and filter out everything else?
- Can you move on from setbacks and misfortune, such as errors, defeat and injury? Or would you dwell on such things, beat yourself up, and become despondent?
- Do you perform with an 'in-the-moment' mindset? Or do thoughts get in the road, dragging you away from the task-at-hand and onto other issues?
- Are you able to identify, confront and overcome self-doubt and destructive thinking, particularly before and during competition?
- Do you have a competition plan, including a schedule for your mental preparation?
- Is there a healthy balance between the various aspects of your life? (For example, between sport, family, personal relationships, friends and education).
- When all is said and done, are you in control of your mind? Or is it in control of you?

How did you get on - is your mental game at a good level? Or does it need topped-up? To join up the dots a little, this review process follows on from your initial assessment/*mental game scan* (see Secret 8) and should be conducted on a regular basis - not just when the tank's empty. And, if you find the level is low, take action right away. Top it up with some solid mental training.

Elite athletes do not see the mental game review as a chore, but as a gateway to learning and development, and considerable performance improvement.

Realising that this area of competition preparation is often what separates winners from losers, keeping their mental game topped-up means that they stay ahead of their 'can't be bothered' opponents.

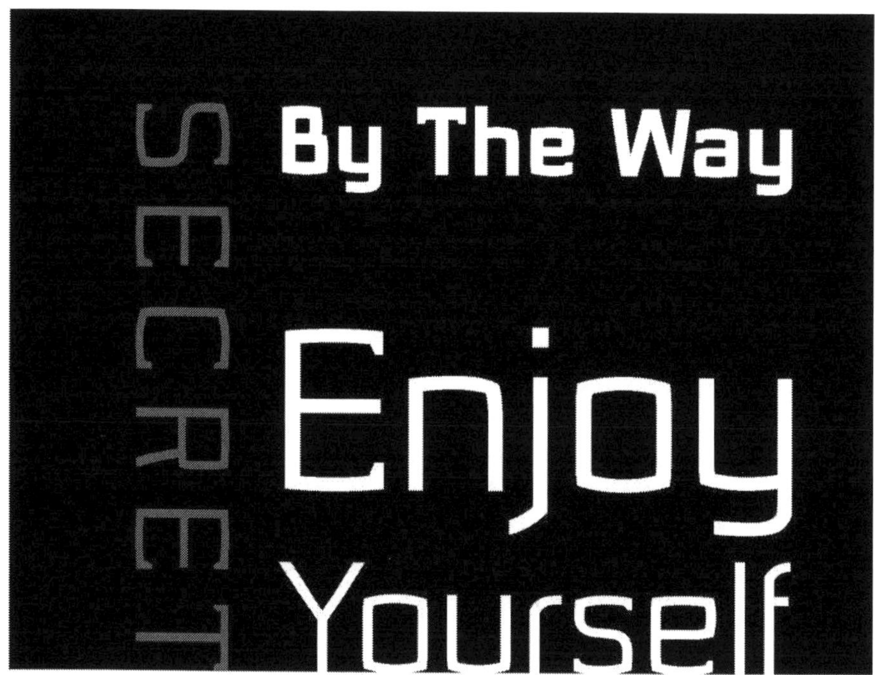

Outstanding athletes enjoy what they do. They love the challenge of improving themselves; of progressing from the base camp of mediocrity to the peak of excellence.

"And what's so surprising about that?" I hear you ask. That those who excel in what they do, take pleasure from what they do.

Well, it's really not as simple as that.

59

While enjoyment and achievement are of course strongly linked, it may surprise you to know that this relationship isn't often emphasised in sporting circles. In fact, it appears to be the very opposite, with many coaches preaching sacrifice and deferred pleasure; that happiness should be put on hold until you have reached your sporting summit.

This is nonsense.

Athletes who do not enjoy what they do, and believe they've made enormous personal sacrifices to go after their dreams, are much more liable to fail and quit. Just listen to what Olympic swimming star, Liam Tancock, has to say about the so-called need to sacrifice things:

> "*Sacrifice seems like such a strong word to me, because I wouldn't say I've sacrificed anything. If I didn't enjoy what I do, I wouldn't do it. I feel I've made the right choices in the way I've lived my life.*" - BBC Sport.

For athletes like Tancock, sport is knitted into the very fabric of their lives. Enjoyment, happiness, success, sport and life all coexist in a dynamic way. This mindset is also adopted by the rugby playing wing, Tommy Bowe:

> "*I play rugby because growing up I had a strong love for the game. I still have that love and am more passionate about it than ever.*" - Personal communication.

Anybody who knows Tommy appreciates his obvious love of life, cheeriness and ability to play with a twinkle in his eye and a smile on his face. He loves his sport, he loves his life. And he possesses an attitude of gratitude based on the fact that he's making a living doing something he enjoys. So while an aspiring athlete must trim the edges off his social life and diet, such tidying-up is seen as a constructive act, *not as* a sacrifice.

I trust you don't consider your pursuit of performance excellence as some kind of chore, as something you're doing while the life you should've been leading is put on hold. This way of thinking will eventually tear you apart. You won't achieve very much, let alone attain sporting supremacy, when what you do feels joyless and a form of purgatory.

If you find this description a little too close to the mark, then you really need to take stock right now. Revisit why you initially played your sport, and find ways to reignite the spark that was once there. As true happiness is always found within the journey, not the destination, you should identify ways to more fully enjoy your training and the whole process of pursuing your dreams.

To help you move away from a 'sacrifice mindset', have a chat with your coach about improving the quality of your training and making it fun. Become connected to what you're doing in training, relish the comradeship of teammates, trainers and coaches, and remain focused on the process of practice.

As Theodore Roosevelt once said, "*Far and away the best prize that life offers is the chance to work hard at work worth doing.*"

The reward is therefore found in the trip and not at the terminus.

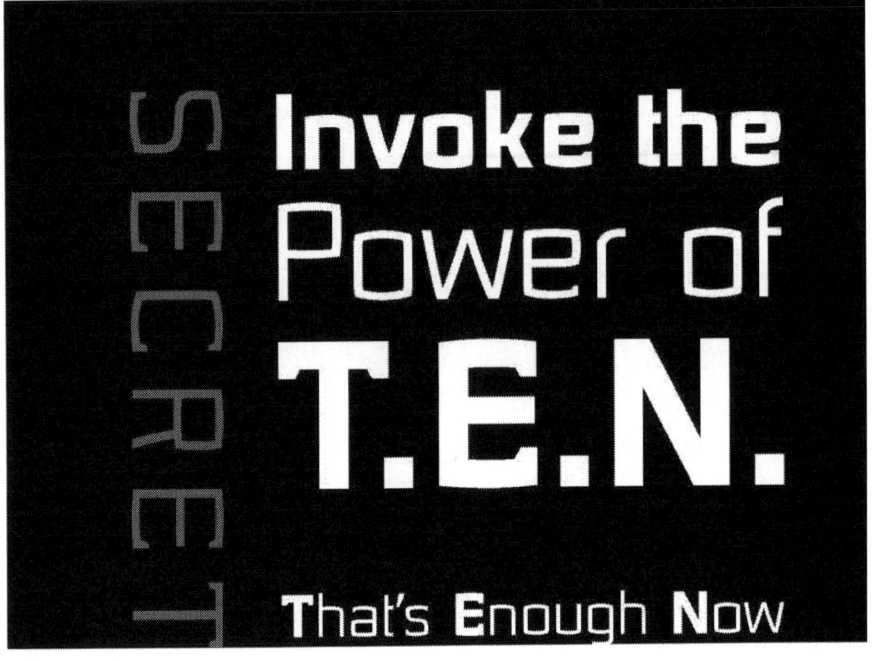

SECRET
Invoke the
Power of
T.E.N.
That's Enough Now

For all of our supposed intelligence, humans are adept at doing the same thing over and over again, expecting different results. We believe that changes in our external world will solve all of our problems and make us happy. But they don't.

I have worked with hundreds and hundreds of athletes, and, to a man and a women, boy and girl, they have all travelled similar routes to see me. Changing coaches, purchasing the latest miracle gadget, or investing in that cutting edge piece of kit, are among their many attempts to turn their performances around. However, in the majority of cases, they found that these external adjustments had short half-lives in terms of their usefulness.

That in the end, there was still something missing.

Yet it was always there, right in front of their noses. Well, *behind* their noses to be exact!

You see, the road to world-class mental toughness, and high level performances, begins with a realisation that it's time to train the brain. Time, in fact, to invoke the **Power of T.E.N.** - a personal pledge to take action now, because doing nothing is changing nothing. T.E.N. stands for: **T**HAT'S **E**NOUGH **N**OW!

Have you reached this stage yet? That enough is enough? That you can't fool yourself any longer? That you know rightly your inner game is letting you down?

If you haven't been engaging in systematic psychological skills training, then I truly hope you are moved to do so by what you've read in this book. It has shown you that your mental game is entirely within your control and that mental toughness can be developed. But you must want it badly, for as with all areas of skill development, you need to do the work. And if you're not sufficiently motivated and committed to learn and practice techniques, then your efforts are likely to fade away.

Far too many athletes sell themselves short when it comes to the mental side of preparation. Some are needlessly fearful about approaching a sport psychologist, while others will drag their feet, putting off the necessary with the feeblest of excuses. If you fall within this group, I suggest you push through the discomfort, leave your procrastinating ways until tomorrow, and do yourself a favour - become mentally tough.

Go for it! You'll be glad you did!

Also available on Amazon from David James Publishing:

Facing Frankenstein

by Dr. Mark S. Elliott

What's mentally demanding about your sport? Is it waiting for kick-off? Making mistakes? Taking a penalty kick in a big match? Receiving a poor decision from the referee? Being close to victory/defeat? Performing in front of the national coach?

For years, athletes have been told that these types of external events and scenarios are why playing sport competitively is mentally challenging. They have been brought up to believe that the sources of their anxieties, distractions and frustrations lie within their sport. However, according to leading sport psychologist, Dr Mark Elliott, this is deceptive and wrong.

At last! A sport psychology book that tells it like it is... In **Facing Frankenstein** you'll discover the TRUTH about why you need to be mentally tough – and it's got nothing to do with sport itself! Instead, you'll find out that you've created a mental monster more cunning, clever and capable than any of your physical opponents. It is your true opponent in sport and you must defeat it! Crucially, the book provides you with the means to do so through its ground-breaking mental training system, The Six Pathways to Mental Toughness programme.

40137028R00116

Made in the USA
Charleston, SC
29 March 2015